The Young Duke

THE EARLY LIFE OF JOHN WAYNE

Howard Kazanjian and Chris Enss

Guilford, Connecticut

Text designed by Cynthia H. Weeks

The Library of Congress has previously catalogued an earlier edition as follows:
Kazanjian, Howard.
  The young Duke : the early life of John Wayne / Howard Kazanjian and Chris Enss. — 1st ed.
     p. cm.
  Filmography:
  Includes bibliographical references and index.
  ISBN: 978-0-7627-3898-4
  1. Wayne, John, 1907-1979. 2. Motion picture actors and actresses—United States—Biography. I. Enss, Chris, 1961- II. Title.
  PN2287.W454K39 2006
  791.4302'8092—dc22
  [B]
                                                     2006011884

ISBN: 978-0-7627-5101-3

Printed in the United States of America
10

CONTENTS

FOREWORD

After performing in more than thirty-three films and TV productions, invariably the first question I'm asked by press and fans alike is, "What was it like to work with John Wayne?"

As we all know, "The Duke" was not only an actor, he was a legend, and he filled his cinematic boots with undeniable impact and elegance. Yes, John Wayne had a unique way of turning all his characters on the big screen into our personal "hero next door."

I had the pleasure of working with "The Duke" in *Rio Lobo,* directed by Howard Hawks.

As I wrote in my autobiography *Surviving Myself:*

John Wayne was a total delight to work with. In a few months I had gone from a half-million-dollar movie to a ten-million-dollar film (remember this was the early seventies), co-starring with one of the world's best-known heroes. It was during the filming of *Rio Lobo* that John Wayne won his Academy Award for *True Grit*—truly a wonderful moment for him. He always told me that the most important thing about acting is to *really* listen. That advice came in handy years later when I worked on a film in Europe where everyone was speaking different languages. Talk about listening for your cue!

The Duke starred in *Rio Lobo* out of respect for Hawks, as they had made many classic films together in the past, but it was rather sad to see this once-renowned director losing his touch. A constant stream of well wishers, supportive friends, and fans of Hawks passed through the set during the entire filming schedule, including the legendary director John Ford and actor Robert Mitchum. A book about Hawks was being written while we shot; the set was hopping, accolades were flying, and I felt honored to be present at what seemed like a giant wrap party for an era gone by.

I only saw the Duke lose his patience once. It was after a gun battle in the saloon where I shot the bad guy and then fainted into the Duke's arms. He was to carry me up the long flight of stairs to exit frame. Remember, John Wayne had had one of his lungs removed due to cancer, so this scene was no easy task for him to perform. I shot the gun, fainted, was caught, and tried to will myself to be light as possible while still playing unconscious. As we ascended the stairs, the Duke's breathing became heavier and heavier . . . I really wasn't sure if he would make it to the top. But he did, and Hawks yelled "cut" . . . only to have the cameraman announce that they didn't film the shot because Hawks forgot to tell him to follow us up the stairs with the camera. With that, the Duke dropped me hard on the floor and stormed off the set swearing that he wouldn't do the scene again. . . . But of course he did. He was a real pro. There were, however, a few things you didn't do with the Duke; you never talked about religion or politics, and you never played cards with him if you expected to win. In my opinion, John Wayne more than deserved his hero status.

What an honor to have worked with this consummate gentleman who blessed millions worldwide with a body of work that will never pale.

—Jennifer O'Neill, actress and author

ACKNOWLEDGMENTS

The authors wish to thank the following organizations and individuals for their generous assistance with this project:

We are indebted to George Ellison at the Special Collections Room of the Glendale Public Library, Chuck Wike at the Glendale Public Library, the Glendale Historical Society, the Lancaster Historical Society, Carolyn Wilson at the John Wayne Birthplace Museum, the staff at the Academy of Motion Picture Arts and Sciences and Academy Foundation and the Margaret Herrick Library, Joanne Drake at the Ronald Reagan Presidential Foundation, the archives department at the *Chicago Tribune*, and Marilyn Carey. Above all, thanks to Erin Turner, the editorial staff, and most especially the exceptional art department at The Globe Pequot Press.

INTRODUCTION

This is the story of the young Duke—John Wayne, the American Star.

John Wayne was the American hero to millions the world over. Men wanted to imitate him, women were in love with him. He endeared himself to every American—rich, poor, workingman, and executive. For more than fifty years he was an American Patriot, handsome actor, a great Western Star, Producer, Director, Father, Husband, Friend, and international icon.

Some refer to the Duke as the fifty-first star on the American flag. He had a unique position in the history of the cinema. Wayne cast a giant shadow over his peers and became the most recognizable face in the world, outshining even some Presidents. To the world, his face was America. To this day he still remains the most popular actor of all time.

— Howard Kazanjian, Hollywood producer

When John Wayne arrived on the Hollywood scene in the mid-1920s he had another name and a plan to become an attorney. The 6-foot-4-inch, brown-haired, blue-eyed University of Southern California football player became perhaps the most recognizable actor in motion-picture history. So clear is the image of Wayne and the heroes he portrayed that few can separate the man from his onscreen personalities.

John Wayne was strong willed and confident, and he believed in the ideal of the American cowboy or American soldier— ideals embodied in the bold characters he portrayed, such as Tom Dunson in *Red River* and Major Daniel Kirby in *Flying Leathernecks*. But John Wayne in his youth was more quiet, reserved, and reluctant to be the center of attention. His gentler, unassuming traits made the people he played more complicated and therefore more real.

Wayne was easy-going, honest, and completely without guile—qualities that attracted studios to him and made him a favorite to work with among his peers. He had millions of admirers that never missed seeing his pictures. They helped to make him the nation's number-one box-office attraction for several years. From his first leading role in *The Big Trail* in 1930, to his final performance in *The Shootist* in 1976, he was a Hollywood superstar.

Though Wayne played many parts in all types of movies, audiences mostly associated him with the part of an American cowboy. Wayne was proud of that. "After all, they shaped my early career," he told a reporter for the *Saturday Evening Post* in 1970. His deep respect for the Western genre could be seen in his performances. He said:

Westerns are folklore, just the same as the Iliad is, and folklore is international. Our Westerns have the same appeal in Germany and

Japan and South America and Greece that they have in our country. But don't ever think they're fool-proof, either. It takes good men to make good Westerns. And besides that, they're fun. I like making Westerns.

Wayne never regarded himself as having any particular appeal. Director John Ford is credited with seeing the possibilities in him and pushing the reluctant Wayne toward certain success. The combination of Ford's drive and Wayne's persona clicked through the twenty-one movies they made together. But Wayne's popularity was not just a by-product of the directors and studios and scripts. The quiet actor had a unique, confident style that transcended the simple cowboy pictures of his early years and also a humanity that made real the epic roles he played years later. He described himself as a "reactor" rather than an actor and prided himself on portraying real people. "What I do best is sell sincerity," he once said. "And I've been selling the hell out of that ever since I started."

At times Wayne's personal life was as well publicized as his professional life. Newspapers and entertainment magazines not only covered the good news of the birth of his seven children (he had four children with his first wife, Josephine Saenz, and three with his third wife, Pilar Pallete), but also reported on his failed marriages and youthful indiscretions. Periodicals that featured articles about John Wayne always sold well. He appeared on the cover of *Life* magazine three times.

Wayne was devoted to the craft of filmmaking and wanted to share the experience with his seven children. His family regularly joined him on the set of his films and acted opposite him in a few as well. His second wife, Chata Bauer, said he was "one of the few people who was always interested in the business no matter where he was or who he was with." It was that driven attitude and focus that made Wayne the icon he continues to be.

Wayne's talent was recognized with numerous awards and the accolades of his peers for his onscreen performances and off-screen achievements. In 1950 when he was honored with a square at Grauman's Chinese Theatre in Hollywood shortly after he was nominated for an Academy Award for best actor in the movie *Sands of Iwo Jima*, the sand used in the cement to make the square was brought in from Iwo Jima. Elizabeth Taylor said when testifying before congress in favor of the Medal of Honor he was awarded, "He gave the whole world the image of what an American should be."

John Wayne passed away on June 11, 1979, when he was seventy-two years old. Upon his death, Ronald Reagan penned a tribute, which read in part:

> We called him DUKE, and he was every bit the giant off screen he was on. Everything about him—his stature, his style, his convictions—conveyed enduring strength, and no one who observed his struggle in those final days could doubt that strength was real. Yet there was more. To my wife, Nancy, "Duke Wayne was the most gentle, tender person I ever knew."

Wayne is buried at the Pacific View Memorial Park in Newport Beach, California. When asked how he wanted to be remembered he replied, *"Feo, Fuerte y Formal"*—Spanish for "He was ugly, strong, and had dignity."

The Young Duke: The Early Life of John Wayne is the story of how a boy from Iowa grew up to win the cinematic West and then pushed movie goers beyond the Pecos. It's the story of the people and circumstances that influenced his young career and the decisions that led to the various roles he assumed, both on and off the screen.

———

"SOMETIMES KIDS ASK ME WHAT A PRO IS.
I JUST POINT TO THE DUKE."

— *Actor Steve McQueen*

BECOMING DUKE

A tall, lanky fourteen-year-old boy sat in the center row of a crowded theatre. His eyes were transfixed on the action on the giant screen in front of him. A piano player to the right of the stage pounded out frantic music that mimicked the events unfolding before him.

A band of warring Indians chased a lone, horse-drawn wagon over rocks and brush. The driver struggled in vain to maintain control of the horses. A rogue arrow hit him in the back, and he rolled off the top of the wagon. The vehicle bounced over a log on the side of the road and with the exception of a three-year-old boy, all of the passengers were thrown. The spooked team of horses pulling the wagon raced toward a jagged cliff.

Marion (Duke) Morrison as a senior in high school. *(From the "Stylus" Yearbook, Glendale Union High School, courtesy of the Special Collections Room, Glendale Public Library, Glendale, California)*

The craggy-faced cowboy Harry Carey, burst onto the chaotic scene, spurring his ride toward the out-of-control wagon. Just before he caught up to the vehicle he fired a few rounds of bullets at the Indians fast on his trail. They dispersed leaving the hero free to save a life. With no thought for his personal safety, he leapt onto the back of the crazed team pulling the wagon. In a matter of moments, he reached the reins and slowed the animals to a stop.

The boy inside the wagon hugged Carey's neck. The piano player's tune lightened, echoing the sentiment behind the child's gratitude. The audience breathed a sigh of relief. Some even applauded the spectacular rescue.

Marion Robert Morrison, the teen in the middle of the enthusiastic movie-goers was mesmerized by what he'd just seen. The silent film *Desperate Trails* could not have been any more compelling. Marion exited the Glendale theatre, his mind still riding the range with his idol Harry Carey. A longing for a Wild West adventure gave his every step purpose, like thousands of cowboys before him, celluloid or otherwise.

Molly Brown Morrison wanted her son to be a respectable attorney—successful in the area of business and finance. She wanted him to be aggressive, tough, and frugal. She wanted him to be the opposite of his father. Clyde Morrison possessed a kind, generous spirit that his wife mistook for foolish sentimentality. Molly always wanted more than Clyde had to offer.

Marion entered the world on May 26, 1907, in Winterset, Iowa. From the moment the 13-pound boy was born he struggled to find a place in his mother's heart. He was the light of his father's life and Molly resented him for it. She cared for him, fed and changed him like a mother should, but his appearance and mannerisms were too much like Clyde's to suit her.

She had reluctantly given her first son her father's name, Robert, for his middle name; however, when Marion was almost four years old, Molly decided to change it. She explained to the child that she wanted her next son to have the name instead. Marion Robert Morrison was renamed Marion Michael Morrison. His brother, born in December 1911, was called Robert. Although the change in his middle name was hurtful, his first name created more problems for him. His peers made fun of him for having what they perceived to be a girl's name, and he ended up in many fights over his handle.

Clyde, a clerk at a pharmacy, tried desperately to make up for Molly's shortcomings with Marion. He showered his son with affection and protected him from his mother's frequent

Marion Morrison's birthplace in Winterset, Iowa, now maintained as a museum.
(*Courtesy of the John Wayne Birthplace Museum*)

outbursts of anger. When Clyde and Molly weren't squabbling
over her treatment of Marion, they were bickering over Clyde's
lack of on-the-job ambition.

Determined to have the affluent, aristocratic lifestyle she
always dreamed of, Molly attempted to mold Clyde into an
entrepreneur. After months of persuasion, Clyde gave into her
demands that he buy his own pharmacy in order to better himself
and his family. Molly scrimped and saved until enough money
was set aside for the couple to purchase a business in 1910.

At the Morrison's pharmacy in Earlham, Iowa, in addition to the various patent medicines for sale, customers could purchase paint, wallpaper, and other household supplies. Clyde had a winning way with customers that guaranteed repeat business. Molly used a portion of the store's profits to build a spacious, two-story Victorian home. It seemed that she finally had everything she longed for, but none of the improvements in her life changed her critical attitude. She persisted in complaining about her lack of social standing and berated Clyde for extending credit to "ne'er-do-wells with no intention of paying off their debts."

Molly and Clyde's behavior blanketed Marion's childhood in despair and worry evidenced by his inability to sleep at night and his hyperactivity during the day. He became a shy loner, spending a great deal of time out of his parents' house and only coming home when he was hungry. Clyde recognized how withdrawn and anxious Marion was becoming and sought to help his eldest son by teaching him how to play football.

Clyde had excelled at the sport in high school and had been rewarded with a scholarship to attend college. He believed football could give Marion confidence and a sense of purpose. He helped organize a group of neighborhood players and served as coach for his son's school team. Marion was a natural athlete, and his father beamed with pride watching him play. Molly was unimpressed and mother and child grew even further apart.

In 1914, Clyde's health began failing and doctors suggested he move to a drier climate to improve his condition. After selling the house and business in Iowa, the Morrisons relocated to Palmdale, California, where Clyde purchased several acres of land with the idea of becoming a farmer. Molly was appalled at the notion and disappointed that she had to leave her lovely home in Earlham to live in what she viewed as a dilapidated shack in the middle of the desert.

While Clyde tried to prove himself to his wife and transform his fields of rock and dry soil into a crop of corn, Marion explored his new surroundings. He hiked through the valley and studied the creatures that inhabited the area. He also taught himself to ride one of the two plow horses that his father kept. After his father showed him how to use a gun, Marion would ride off on one of the animals and go hunting for wild game.

Marion and his brother Robert learned to adapt to life on an emerging farm, but Molly put forth minimal effort. The boys would fall asleep to the sound of their parents arguing about their financial state and depressed living conditions. After a two-year struggle to make the farm work, Clyde finally submitted to Molly's complaints and sold the land. The Morrisons moved to Glendale, California, and Clyde again took a position as a clerk at a pharmacy. His boys adjusted nicely to life in the suburbs and for a short while Molly's disposition improved.

Duke's mother, Mary (Molly) Brown Morrison. *(Courtesy of the Special Collections Room, Glendale Public Library, Glendale, California)*

Young Marion (Duke) Morrison.
(Courtesy of the Special Collections
Room, Glendale Public Library, Glendale,
California)

It seemed that things were finally going well for young Marion. The nine-year-old boy thrived in the Southern California community. He joined the Boy Scouts and the YMCA and got involved in many after-school projects. He was even able to take on part-time jobs to help supplement the family's income. He made many friends and managed to talk his parents into letting him have a dog. Marion and his Airedale, Duke, were inseparable.

Duke followed Marion as he worked his paper route and delivered medicine and supplies from the pharmacy to neighborhood residents. The boy and his dog would pass by the local fire station on their daily rounds and visit with the firefighters on duty. The men referred to Marion as Big Duke and the Airedale as Little Duke. The nickname stuck, and the handle Marion, which he had always disliked, was replaced with one more fitting his independent personality.

In spite of the early improvement in the family life after they had relocated to Glendale, Molly regretted ever leaving Iowa and repeatedly threatened to abandon Clyde and return to the Midwest. Part of her frustration lay in the fact that Clyde was an easy touch for anyone needing a handout, and the Morrisons found themselves in desperate financial situations. Their money woes forced them to move frequently—always into less expensive housing. Clyde moved his family eight times in the first nine years they resided in the area and each house was more run-down than the next. Molly gave voice to her disapproval every chance she had, and the arguments at home worsened.

Duke, as he now preferred to be called, continued to avoid being around his parents as much as possible. When he wasn't at school or working, he was holed up at a nearby library poring over history books and classical literature. The long hours he spent learning about Shakespeare, the Old West, the United States, and the world helped make him an exceptional student. His teachers noted that he was a quiet, intelligent pupil who was serious about his studies.

Duke was also well liked by his peers. Throughout his Glendale Union High School career he served as either vice president or president of his class. Outside of football, his favorite extracurricular activity was drama. As a member of the Thespian Society, Duke performed in a variety of plays from *Henry VIII* to *First Lady of the Land*. One of the many after-school jobs he held was working as a handbill deliverer for the Palace Grand Movie Theatre in Glendale. When he wasn't on the job or studying, he was at the Palace.

Three or four times a week Duke would escape into the world of motion picture cowboys and Indians by watching films starring his idols, Tom Mix and Harry Carey. "I understand my fans," Duke would admit later in his life. "I had my idols too. I guess watching famous movie stars gave me some inspiration."

As a freshman in high school (1922), Duke Morrison took to the football field. *(From the "Stylus" Yearbook, Glendale Union High School, courtesy of the Special Collections Room, Glendale Public Library, Glendale, California)*

With the junior class (1923) at Glendale Union High School, Duke Morrison is in the second row, fourth from the left. (From the "Stylus" Yearbook, Glendale Union High School, courtesy of the Special Collections Room, Glendale Public Library, Glendale, California)

Duke Morrison (front row, third from the right) with the 1924 Glendale Union High School football team. *(From the "Stylus" Yearbook, Glendale Union High School, courtesy of the Special Collections Room, Glendale Public Library, Glendale, California)*

Soon Duke was not content to enjoy just the finished movie, and he often made his way onto the lot of the Kalem Motion Picture Company. The successful silent-movie studio was located several miles from the Morrisons' home, but Duke didn't mind the trek. He was enamored with the process and with the actors and stunt performers. He got to see the swashbuckling hero Douglas Fairbanks Sr. and *Perils of Pauline* star Helen Holmes at work. Duke considered Fairbanks to be the finest actor of the time and would practice the death-defying stunts he saw him do. Helen Holmes captured Duke's adolescent fancy and for years he measured every girl he met against her standard.

In May 1925 he graduated from high school. Duke's interest in film and acting had not diminished over time, but that ambition was momentarily overshadowed by his determination to join the Navy and become an officer. Perhaps the notion of sailing out to sea and away from the turbulent upbringing was appealing to him, but Duke's application to the Naval Academy was denied.

As Duke considered his alternatives, the battle between his mother and father raged on. They disagreed about what college their son would attend, if he could attend, and what he would study. Molly wanted Duke to go into law. Clyde wanted him to pursue sports. A football scholarship to the University of Southern California made both their plans possible. In the fall of 1925, eighteen-year-old Marion Michael Morrison enrolled at USC.

Duke Morrison (third from the left) as part of a stage crew for a Glendale Union High School Production. *(From the "Stylus" Yearbook, Glendale Union High School, courtesy of the Special Collections Room, Glendale Public Library, Glendale, California)*

Duke Morrison (fourth from the right) looking fetching as part of the Glendale Union High School football team's mock fashion show. *(From the "Stylus" Yearbook, Glendale Union High School, courtesy of the Special Collections Room, Glendale Public Library, Glendale, California)*

Duke's freshman year was a busy time. Not only was he taking a full schedule of classes and practicing with the Trojan team, he was working two jobs to help pay the living expenses not covered by the scholarship. Duke was also a member of Sigma Chi fraternity. He was warmly accepted by the other members of the house, and he thrived on the camaraderie.

Just before he began his second year at college, his parents' relationship came to an end. After more than twenty years of marriage, Clyde and Molly separated. Molly filed for divorce on the grounds of desertion. Clyde did not fight her. The divorce was finalized on February 20, 1930.

Marion (Duke) Morrison took the field as a USC Trojan in 1925, intending to study law. *(From the "Stylus" Yearbook, Glendale Union High School, courtesy of the Special Collections Room, Glendale Public Library, Glendale, California)*

Duke managed to remove himself emotionally from his parents' divorce by losing himself in his work, school, and football. He was handsome, smart, unassuming, and easy to get along with—one of the most popular students on campus. It also made him quite a catch for the women there as well. Duke dated frequently, but only when he wasn't in training for a big game. USC football coach, Howard Jones, imposed strict rules about such frivolity prior to major competitions. Duke respected and admired Jones and made a point to live by the guidelines the players were given. Under Coach Jones's instruction, Duke proved to be an integral part of the team.

No father was more proud of his son than Clyde Morrison. He was at every game Duke played, and Duke was relieved to see his father happy at last. Duke's brother moved to Long Beach with Molly, and Duke had limited contact with his mother and Robert. Molly never attended any of Duke's football games.

Tickets for the 1926–1927 USC football season were a hot commodity. Film stars and state politicians scrambled to get box seats for the heated competitions with rival universities. Among the motion-picture celebrities interested in seeing the winning Trojan team play was cowboy star Tom Mix. Mix struck a bargain with Coach Jones, promising players summer jobs at Fox Films Corporations in exchange for box seats. At the end of the semester, a couple of players took Tom Mix up on his offer; Duke Morrison was one of them.

It was Mix's hat that first caught Duke's attention when he met the actor. The white ten-gallon headpiece was larger than any he'd ever seen. The rest of the cowboy star's outfit was colorful and grand, as well. He looked like one of his on-screen personas. After giving the hired hands a tour of the studio and discussing the next football season, he introduced them to the head of the building and prop department. Duke and his fellow classmate were put to work moving sets and furniture.

Mix caught up with the pair before the end of the first day and suggested they consider working as extras in his next western production. "You're both splendid-looking men," he told them. "I think there's a future in pictures for both of you."

Duke had no idea how right Tom Mix would be.

————

BIOGRAPHY OF JOHN WAYNE

(Starred in Paramount's "Shepherd of the Hills")
Paramount, JP Burkhart – November 1940

The following biography of John Wayne was one of the items circulated by Paramount publicity staff about the new Western Shepherd of the Hills, Wayne's first major role since the success of Stagecoach. Some of the information contained in the biography about Wayne is incorrect, but accuracy wasn't the studio's first concern.

John Wayne, handsome young he-man of the screen, is one of Hollywood's busiest actors these days.

Starting with *"The Dark Command,"* which he made for his home studio, he has been continuously before the cameras for a year, going from one picture to another with seldom more than a Sunday intervening.

His last three productions are the biggest he has made in his career, indicating his growing popularity. According to recent surveys, he is picking up favor with fans throughout the country more rapidly than any other player in pictures.

Wayne has waited a long time to reach the goal that comes to some lucky ones almost overnight. It was nearly nine years ago that he suddenly was plucked from a job as property boy with John Ford at the Old Fox studio to be the leading man in *"The Big Trail."* This was a super-gigantic film of those days, directed by Raoul Walsh, but somehow it didn't quite come off. Wayne and Marguerite Churchill, whom the picture was expected to establish as stars, suffered as a consequence in their professional careers.

Miss Churchill played in a few more pictures, and then retired after she married George O'Brien to devote all her attention to being a mother and a housewife.

Wayne was dropped by the studio that "discovered" him and eked out a meager career in westerns for poverty row producers. Gradually, he built up a following among the younger generation and eventually Republic, the largest of the independents, signed him on a five-year contract.

He was still doing westerns, but better ones and his following among fans who dote on hard-riding, fast-shooting spies of the range expanded tremendously. But still he was getting no place, so far as stardom was concerned.

Ford, who had originally recommended him for "The Big Trail" role, decided to take a hand and borrowed the young actor for "Stagecoach." Wayne soared to overnight popularity in that and came close to winning an Academy Award for his fine performance.

But no studio sought his services and he went back to making westerns for Republic. Two years after "Stagecoach," Ford decided to prime the pump again and chose Wayne for a co-starring role with Thomas Mitchell in "The Long Voyage Home." As a result of the publicity he received while making that picture, other studios remembered that they had intended to do something with this strapping, ingratiating young man before, and half a dozen of them started bidding for his services.

The day he finished with Ford, he went over to Universal to co-star with Marlene Dietrich in "Seven Sinners." Henry Hathaway, Paramount director and producer, also put in a bid for Wayne for the role of Young Matt in "Shepherd of the Hills," and while he was still playing love scenes with Dietrich, he was being measured for costumes for the Harold Bell Wright epic.

The day he completed his "Seven Sinners" assignment, he hurried off to Big Bear Valley in the San Bernardino Mountains to report to Hathaway who is filming his picture in Technicolor entirely on location.

Wayne regards *"Shepherd of the Hills"* as his most important picture yet, and believes now that he is through with typical westerns for good. He has half a dozen pictures lined up for future production and it looks like he'll keep on working steadily without a break for another year or two. He graduated into the picture industry from the University of Southern California, where he played tackle with the famous Trojans.

A broken ankle halted his gridiron career, and while it was growing strong again he got a studio job and never went back to school.

Born in Winterset, Iowa, Wayne came to California with his family at the age of two and grew up on a ranch near Lancaster. There he learned to ride and to handle himself in all sorts of difficult situations, a circumstance that stood him in good stead in his "quickie" days when he had to do all his own stunts.

He is married to Josephine Saenz and they have three children, the oldest not yet six years old.

He is one of the tallest men in pictures, towering some six feet three and three-fourths inches in his socks. Cowboy boots added about four inches to that. He weighs a trifle over 200 pounds, and is reputed to be one of the hardest punchers in pictures.

Hunting is his favorite sport, which he's devoting his three days off to, although he can't get too far away from the location as he's subject to call on two hours notice.

"But even so, I'm thoroughly enjoying my unexpected holiday and it seems as good to me as a month off," he says.

On July 18, 1941, Paramount Pictures released a film starring John Wayne, Betty Field and Harry Carey entitled *"Shepherd of the Hills."* Press packets about the movie and its cast were sent to theatre owners, newspaper and radio reporters, industry leaders. The press packets contained still photographs from the film and biographies about the actors and the roles they were playing.

"WAYNE IS UNDERRATED. HE'S AN AWFULLY GOOD ACTOR: HE HOLDS A THING TOGETHER; HE GIVES IT A SOLIDITY AND HONESTY, AND HE CAN MAKE A LOT OF THINGS BELIEVABLE."

— *Director Howard Hawks*

THE BIG
TRAIL

Cowboy star Tom Mix hung precariously from a steel cable
stretched across jagged rocks and the fast moving rapids of
the Royal Gorge in Colorado. Hand-over-hand he inched his
way over the rough waters below toward a recess in the mountains on the other side. A trio of bandits stood near the ledge,
drinking and laughing, unaware that Mix had reached the massive boulder directly below them. Mix quietly scaled the moun-
tainside and eventually ended up behind the men where he
ordered them to drop their weapons and throw up their hands.
The leader of the bad guys quickly reached for his gun and the
other two followed suit. Mix gunned them down before they
fired a single shot. One of the men struggled to sit up and cock
his gun. KABLAAM! Mix shot him again. This time the man
stayed down and didn't move.

A boisterous movie director yelled "cut!" The cameras stopped rolling and Mix hurried off to speak with the film crew. The gunshot victims got to their feet. One of the wounded film extras removed the cowboy hat from his head and beat the dust off of his pants and chaps. He glanced down at a train traveling along the water's edge hundreds of feet below. The view was breathtaking, and Duke Morrison felt privileged to be there.

———

The release of the movie *The Great K&A Train Robbery* in the late 1920s marked the beginning of Duke's fifty-plus years in the movies. Throughout the summer of 1926 he worked at Fox studios in the property department and appeared as a bit player in a few films. He doubled for silent screen actor Francis X. Bushman in *Brown of Harvard*, portrayed a guard in the historic epic *Bardelys the Magnificent*, and was a Scottish soldier in the war drama *Annie Laurie*. He earned $35 a week for the variety of services he offered.

Shortly after the release of *The Great K&A Train Robbery*, Duke entered his sophomore year at the University of Southern California. He had no plans to enter into motion pictures full-time; he was a law student and a Trojan football player who dreamed of being an All-American.

When the driven athlete wasn't at football practice or doing homework, he was at the beach. Duke and his fraternity brothers liked to play in the waves of the ocean, diving into

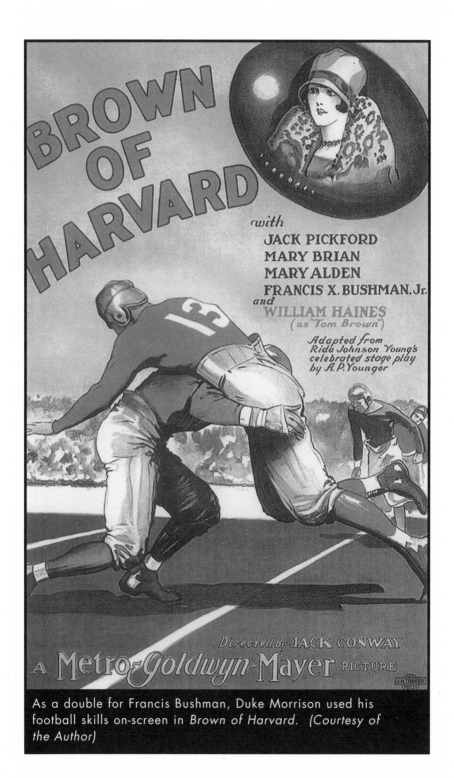

As a double for Francis Bushman, Duke Morrison used his football skills on-screen in *Brown of Harvard*. (Courtesy of the Author)

the curl of the water and riding the waves to shore. Duke learned the hard way that the activity was not without its hazards. He sustained a serious injury body surfing in the choppy surf at Huntington Beach. A strong wave forced his frame down on the sea floor a few inches from shore, dislocating his right shoulder. His future as an interior linesman for USC was in question.

Duke tried to stifle the pain while training and running plays, but the damage was significant. His performance on the field suffered as a result, and by the end of his second year in college, he had lost his place on the team.

Being cut from the Trojans had far-reaching implications. The scholarship he was receiving for playing football was cut as well. For awhile Duke managed to survive at USC without his scholarship. He took on several part-time jobs including working for the phone company and washing dishes, but the pressure to make ends meet was overwhelming. Duke's father contributed to his son's living expenses when he could, but there was not enough to keep him in school.

In May 1927, Duke decided to abandon any thought of furthering his education, and against his father's wishes, he left USC. Leaving football proved to be a life-changing experience. Without it Duke wasn't completely sure of his capabilities. Despondent and nursing a broken heart after the relationship with his steady girl ended, he went searching for his life's new calling. He'd heard from friends that San Francisco had a lot to offer so he made his way there.

After two weeks of job searching in Northern California with no success, Duke's snuck on board the steamship the SS *Malolo*, headed to Hawaii. The ill-conceived venture ended with the stowaway's arrest. The authorities decided not to press charges and sent Duke back to Los Angeles on the evening train.

Back on his home turf, Duke considered his options. He decided to approach the head of the property department at Fox studios about hiring him on again. From 1927 to 1930, Duke learned the art of propping a movie. He worked closely with set designers, cinematographers, and costumers to perfect the overall look of a film. The education was invaluable and served as an important foundation for the opportunities yet to come in Duke's life.

Duke propped for such directing giants as Raoul Walsh (*Desperate Journey, White Heat),* Howard Hawks (*Red River, El Dorado),* and John Ford (*The Quiet Man, The Man Who Shot Liberty Valance).* The aggressive, opinionated Ford wielded a significant influence over Duke's career.

As a fan of Harry Carey, Duke was familiar with John Ford, recognizing him as the director of several Carey Westerns. The two met in 1928 on the set of the film *Mother Machree*, where Duke's job on the picture was to herd a gaggle of geese in the

Duke Wayne looked the part of a Western hero by 1927.
(Courtesy of the Academy of Motion Picture Arts and Sciences)

direction of the action once shooting began. Much to the director's chagrin, Duke could not get the birds to cooperate, and Ford wasn't shy about verbalizing his displeasure. He yelled and cursed at Duke, whose response was equally volatile. The confrontation subsided once Ford recognize Duke from the USC team. He quizzed him about being a football player and then challenged him to block a tackle. The two worked out their aggressions in an abbreviated scrimmage. The result was a mutual respect and friendship that lasted more than forty years.

Duke focused on becoming an expert in the area of propping and scene continuity. When needed, he filled in as a scene extra. He appeared in many films as a face in a crowd, was a member of various angry mobs, and was a dancer in a couple of musical comedies. He even took a turn as a stunt double on the movie *Variety*. Although he enjoyed the time in front of the camera, he much preferred working behind the scenes.

"In those days, you could operate in every department of pictures," Duke said in an interview with *Modern Screen Magazine* in 1968. "You didn't need a union card. I was a carpenter. I was a juicer. I rigged lights. I helped build sets. Carried props. Hauled furniture. I got to know the nuts and bolts of making pictures." He concluded, "More importantly, I was made to feel like I belonged."

Among the myriad reasons Duke did not entertain thoughts of pursuing acting was that he believed he looked "ugly" on film. John Ford did not agree. In fact, he felt Duke's unique looks and well-proportioned frame were the right ones for a film he was doing entitled *Salute*. Ford convinced Duke to appear in the movie and portray an Annapolis graduate and ex-football player for the Navy who was now serving on a war ship. It was Duke's first real speaking role.

In the film, Duke worked alongside another USC football player, Ward Bond. Bond was a big, 220-pound man with broad shoulders and hard, rugged features. Duke didn't like Bond at first. He had a massive ego and a bad habit of speaking before he thought. However, his forthrightness and candor eventually won Duke over. By the time shooting on the film was complete, the two were the best of friends. They would appear in more than twenty-five movies together.

After a long day on the set, Duke, Bond, and Ford played cards, sailed on Ford's boat, and drank each other under the table. Ford became not only Duke's friend, but also his acting coach and mentor. Duke lovingly referred to him as "Pappy" or "Coach." The three worked together on Ford's next picture, *Men Without Women*. Duke's role as a lieutenant in the Navy was bigger than his previous one and included Duke's first close-up.

Duke did double duty on the submarine-themed film. The script called for several sailors, trapped in the doomed vessel, to escape their death by being shot out of the torpedo tubes. Trained divers were on hand to rescue the actors once they made it to the surface, but still the men playing the sailors refused to take part in the stunt because the conditions of the water off the coast of Catalina were too dangerous. Ford disregarded their warning and prevailed upon Duke to do the stunt. Duke eagerly obliged.

Once the shooting for *Men Without Women* was complete, Duke returned contentedly to propping Fox films, but the experience on the picture had proved Duke had the makings of a quality of stuntman. It also ignited his passion for film acting.

Duke would not actively seek out roles to play, but he wouldn't turn down any part offered. He didn't have to wait long before such a request for his services came from director Raoul Walsh. Walsh was searching for a tough, good-looking actor for a Western he was making called *The Big Trail*. After Walsh talked with John Ford about the film and his idea of the leading man, Ford suggested he cast Duke in the picture.

Walsh had seen Duke around the lot and agreed that his physical presence was perfect, but he knew the studio executives would insist on a screen test. Walsh's casting director approached Duke and asked him if he'd be interested in "slipping on a pair of buckskin pants and making a test just for fun." Duke answered with an enthusiastic "sure" and set off to read for the part.

Walsh felt Duke came across on camera as vibrant and capable, "a natural for the role of a leader of an ill-fated wagon train headed West." Studio executives objected only to Duke Morrison's name, which they felt didn't sound American enough.

For more than an hour Fox executives, along with Raoul Walsh, discussed what name better suited their film's new star. Walsh suggested "Wayne" as a last name. After the name John was mentioned it was quickly decided that Duke Morrison would be called John Wayne. In addition to an improved handle, Wayne got a raise. His salary was increased from $35 to $75 a week.

The day Duke was offered the part in *The Big Trail* he began training for the role. He took acting, voice, and horseback riding lessons. He learned to shoot, rope, and throw a knife. When principal photography began, he was well prepared to star in what Fox was calling "the most impressive western ever made."

The Big Trail, starring Marguerite Churchill and Tyrone Power Sr., cost $1 million to make and was released in October of 1930. The film made its national debut at Grauman's Chinese Theatre in Hollywood, California, and the studio supplied Duke with two guest passes to the premiere. He offered his mother and father the tickets and hoped they would agree to set aside their past differences for one evening and attend. Molly refused and insisted the tickets should go to her and Duke's brother. When Duke tried to reason with her, she issued an ultimatum: She would not go unless Duke gave her both of the tickets.

Recognizing the difficult situation his son was in, Clyde told him that his feelings would not be hurt if he went along with his mother's request. Duke decided not to give into Molly's

Publicity still featuring a new Western hero.
(Courtesy of the Academy of Motion Picture
Arts and Sciences)

Co-starring Ed Brendel and Marilyn Harris, *The Big Trail* was not a big commercial success, but it launched John Wayne's career as an actor. *(Courtesy of the Academy of Motion Picture Arts and Sciences)*

demand. Clyde and his second wife, Florence Davis Morrison, acted as Duke's escorts at the event.

Wayne delivered a solid performance in the film; he had even done his own stunts. A review of the picture in the October 26, 1930, edition of the *New York Times* noted that "Mr. Wayne acquitted himself with no little distinction. His performance is pleasingly natural."

The film itself was a box office flop, but the poor ticket sales did not adversely affect Wayne's budding career. *The Big Trail* launched him as an actor. Fox quickly signed the prop man

turned actor to a contract and starred Wayne in two more
pictures.

However, Wayne was less than pleased about the quality of
work Fox offered him. After Walsh's epic Western, the first film
he did was an absurd comedy called *Girls Demand Excitement*.
Wayne played the part of a hard-working college student whose
dislike of women attending college weakens due to the amorous
adventures with a spoiled socialite coed. He cringed at the
thought of his involvement in a movie he felt was "substandard."

Will Rogers, Fox's most bankable star at the time, noticed
Wayne's discontented air and asked him what the problem was.
Wayne explained that the part was not a good one.

"So what," Rogers said with a grin. "You're working, aren't
you? That's the important thing. So get at it and quit griping."
Wayne did just that. Later on in his life he admitted that
Girls Demand Excitement was the worst film he ever made.
However, the advice to keep working became part of his
philosophy.

Unbeknownst to John Wayne at the time, John Ford was
furious with him for starring in *The Big Trail*. He had suggested
Wayne for the film, but he had underestimated his appeal, and
Ford saw Wayne's rise to fame under the guidance of a director
other than himself as a betrayal of sorts. Prior to Wayne being
cast in the film, Ford saw himself as the talent who should be
nurturing Wayne's career in order to star his protégé in a picture when he felt the time was right. As punishment for his

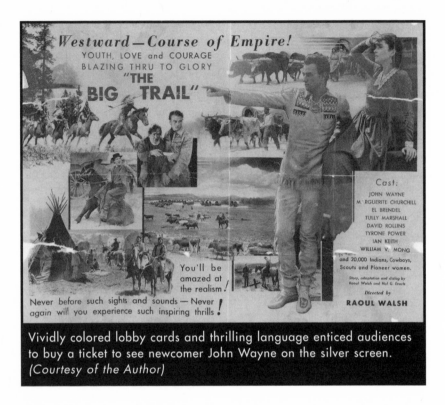

Vividly colored lobby cards and thrilling language enticed audiences to buy a ticket to see newcomer John Wayne on the silver screen. (Courtesy of the Author)

success, Ford refused to speak to Wayne. Wayne didn't press the issue. He decided instead to leave Ford alone with his irrational animosity.

Wayne followed up his role in *Girls Demand Excitement* with a lead in *Three Girls Lost* opposite Loretta Young. He did his best with the gentlemanly part given to him. Critics panned the film but singled out Wayne's performance as "showing much promise." However, the favorable remarks Wayne received from critics and moviegoers were not enough to persuade Fox executives to keep him under contract. An actor's worth was based on the amount of money he earned for the

The Big Trail may not have been "the most important picture ever produced" but it produced one of the most important stars of all time. *(Courtesy of the Author)*

studio, and Wayne's last three movies had not taken in as much as they cost to make. Consequently, he was let go.

It was 1931. The Great Depression meant that jobs in many fields were hard to come by, and the motion-picture industry was no exception. Wayne was momentarily troubled by his circumstances. It was the same feeling he had had after being cut from the USC football team.

John Ford, Wayne's one-time mentor and drinking buddy, was still under contract at Fox. The studio executives considered him their top director, and they were thrilled when he agreed to make another Western for them. Ford knew Wayne was unemployed, but didn't even consider him when he started casting the film. He was still holding a grudge and would continue to do so for another seven years.

Harry Cohn and Columbia Pictures came to Wayne's rescue, signing him to a five-year contract. In a short time he was on his way to becoming one of Hollywood's leading B Western stars.

———————

SAMSON OF HOLLYWOOD

John Wayne Needed a Haircut And Became Famous
Elisabeth Goldbeck, *Motion Picture Magazine*—
February 1931

How one young man let his hair grow long before he became a movie star, instead of after, is the surprising story of John Wayne. John is the new Western hero, latest exponent of the rugged type that Gary Cooper made famous.

His first part was the lead in *"The Big Trail"* and there's no use saying that he can't act because he doesn't even have pretensions.

"I knew there was no use trying to act," he said, "because I didn't know a thing about it. But I figured that if they liked me as I am—just being natural—I'd get along all right."

John was born in Iowa. When he was a child, they moved West into the desert for his father's health and he learned to ride Western ponies—the first step toward being a good movie actor.

This photo and article, which appeared with a 1931 article in *Motion Picture Magazine,* confirmed Duke's status as a heartthrob. *(Courtesy of* Motion Picture Magazine*)*

Next they moved to Glendale just a few miles from Hollywood and there he grew up and went to school. After one year at the University of Southern California he applied to the college employment bureau for a summer job, and was sent to the property department of the Fox Studios.

He went back there the next summer and by that time had grown so interested in the film business that after two and a half years in college he decided to stay at Fox—with the secret hope, of course, of some day becoming a director. It never occurred to him that he might be an actor, so he took no precautions against it and the thing happened when he was completely off his guard. It just slipped up on him when he wasn't looking.

One afternoon, when he had been working night and day on "Born Reckless," and hadn't been able to get a haircut for weeks, he was walking across the lot when he met a friend of his with Raoul Walsh, the director. He was introduced and Walsh looked him over carefully, noticed his height and his rangy build, his manly open countenance, and particularly the fringe of dark hair that hung over his collar. He asked John to call at his office the next morning.

John was innocently pleased, but not excited. He knew Walsh had just been entrusted with a few of the Fox millions and was casting for his huge pioneer spectacular *"The Big Trail,"* but that had nothing to do with him. He was going to a fraternity banquet that night, and his only thought was to get to the barbers. He was just going into the shop when his friend caught him.

"Hey! Come out of there!" he shouted. "Whatever you do, don't have your hair cut till you see Mr. Walsh tomorrow."

That was the first inkling John had of what it was all about. He didn't go into the barber shop that night—and he hasn't had a haircut since. What greater success story can the industry offer?

The usual suspense, mystery, and hocus-pocus followed his first visit to Mr. Walsh. Without being at all let in on the secret and at what he considered the risk of losing his job in the property department he was told to go out and practice knife throwing every day. He was given all sorts of screen tests. He was tested for looks, he was tested for voice, for costume, and for presence of mind. They made him make up his own dialogue, which would be a severe ordeal even for a seasoned actor. Feeling that something wonderful was going to happen to him, he went through it all with a great deal of courage and patience.

Then one day, as nonchalantly as possible, Mr. Walsh mentioned to him that he had the lead in *"The Big Trail"* and should prepare to leave for the first location at once.

That was five months ago. What with pep-talks from Mr. Walsh and Tully Marshall, earnest feelings about making good and not disappointing those who had faith in him, and sympathy and cooperation from the whole company, including the horses, John Wayne got through it to the complete satisfaction of everyone. Before it was over he became such an accomplished knife thrower that now he can outline anybody who is silly enough to stand up against a wall. The day I talked to him, he was going out to Central Park to outline a couple of policemen, in an effort to make New York *"Big Trail"* conscious.

I was a little shocked to find an inch or two of hair still waving about his neck. But he put my fears at rest by explaining that they were making him leave it that way so he would look in character during a personal appearance tour through the key cities.

John is just as he looks. Simple and forthright, appreciative and loyal—a good boy, with all the steadfastness that could be expected of a young pioneer, and much more humor. Though he has been a leading man for months, his whole glorious career has taken place out in the open spaces. *"The Big Trail"* was shot entirely on remote and wholesome locations, where actors sometimes become people, so John has known none of the joys and perils of success in Hollywood.

———————

The blond and boyish Clark Twelve-trees, ex-husband of the wistful Helen, the young man who dives out of windows, was with him, calling on a diplomatic mission.

"Here's a story for you," he cried, jumping up in his excitement. "A girl I know has fallen in love with John, just from seeing his picture outside the Roxy. She insists on meeting him. Really! And you'd be amazed, too, if I told you her name. She's a leading woman on Broadway. It's a great story. I can't tell you who she is, but she's playing right on Forty-Fifth Street!"

Smiling rather foolishly, John got up and took Clark to the door, where they made the last sweet arrangements for a romantic meeting.

"I'm at the age," he confessed when he came back, "where I'm very much interested in girls."

But he would say no more. Mr. Wayne is a cautious young man, not to be proved on any subject that he considers in the least incriminating. He has been getting a lot of good advice, and actually taking it, on what is discreet for a rising young star to say, and what is not. So if you can get him to express an opinion on anything or anybody connected with the motion picture business, it will be in a weak and unguarded moment.

As I was leaving, the little Irish chambermaid came in, with sparkling eyes and a smile that would have flattered any man.

"Is that how you affect her?" I asked.

"No," said John. "That's because next week she's going to marry a policeman."

An hour later I saw our young pioneer, arm in arm with a hatless, Titian-haired young lady, strolling through the tides of traffic in Times Square as heedless, as absorbed, as if they were wandering across a prairie. I couldn't be sure, but I think they were coming from Forty-Fifth Street.

"I CAN'T IMAGINE THERE'S ANYONE IN THE COUNTRY WHO DOESN'T KNOW WHO HE IS. KIDS WILL BE TALKING ABOUT HIM LONG AFTER THE REST OF US ARE GONE."

— *Actor Jimmy Stewart*

HOME ON
THE RANGE

The June sun beat savagely down on the Antelope Valley landscape some 100 miles northeast of Los Angeles. John Wayne escorted his ride past a camera crew preparing to film a scene. He walked the horse to a small patch of ground shaded by an outcropping of rock, then he eased the roan around in a quarter turn and squinted hard into the heat waves hovering off the desert floor. The heat was almost unbearable. He removed his six-shooter from its holster and made sure it was fully loaded with bullets.

Wayne wiped the sweat off his brow and stared long into the horizon. In the distance was the distorted image of twenty or more riders fast approaching. The riders were highly skilled cowboys working as film extras—authentic saddle pals that at one time kept a watchful eye over the herds on the wide-open range.

Once miles of fencing had stopped livestock from roaming, the need for the cowboy of old had all but vanished, and by the late 1920s, rodeos and motion pictures were among the only places cowboys could reliably find work. Their talents for bull riding, lassoing and roping, and tying steers were used quite extensively in early Hollywood Westerns. Wayne considered it a privilege to work alongside the last of these true American icons. He adopted their walk and mannerisms and used them to create a persona that ultimately embodied the quintessential Western hero.

"One of the most satisfying things about that time," Wayne shared with *Life* magazine in 1961, "was the camaraderie of the cowboys who worked on those films. They were real cowboys, not actors. . . . These cowboys were the last of their kind. Working in pictures together, they found some kind of solace in just being with each other. I respected them. I listened to their stories and kind of absorbed their culture."

———————

White hat firmly on head, John Wayne looked like a classic cowboy star. *(Courtesy of the Academy of Motion Picture Arts and Sciences)*

Wayne's first experience working with such accomplished rop-ers and riders happened during the filming of *The Big Trail* in 1929. His chance to be surrounded by the genuine article wouldn't come again until 1932 because Columbia Pictures wanted to try Wayne out in more sophisticated roles. Studio president Harry Cohn thought the well-built actor would look just as good in a dinner jacket as he did in a buckskin outfit.

Subsequently Wayne was cast in the refined, romantic com-edy *Men Are Like That* opposite silent-movie star Lara La Plante. Wayne played the debonair soldier Lieutenant Bob Denton, a West Point graduate who breaks up with his girl-friend and is then transferred to an army post in Arizona. The girl eventually marries another soldier and follows her husband to the same post as Wayne's character. Critics called their per-formances "unconvincing," and consequently the film did not do well at the box office.

John Wayne assumed the picture's poor reviews would be the topic of conversation when he was summoned to the office of Columbia Pictures' president, Harry Cohn, shortly after the film's release. He anticipated having to give Cohn a reason for keeping him under contract with the studio. Cohn was indeed upset, but it had nothing to do with Wayne's acting.

Rumors circulating about an affair Wayne was supposedly having with Lara La Plante had reached Cohn. Cohn was in love with La Plante and furious with Wayne. Wayne, who was in love with a young socialite named Josephine Saenz, denied any involvement with the actress. Duke politely explained that he and Lara were simply good friends, but Cohn didn't believe him. He didn't fire Wayne though, choosing instead to keep him on at the studio and make his life at Columbia a living hell.

From 1929 to 1931, Cohn had John Wayne play demeaning, less-than-supporting roles. In the fifth and final movie he did for the studio, entitled *The Drop Kick,* Wayne portrayed a nefarious college football player who sells out his team. Cohn knew that Wayne had been a star football player for the University of Southern California at one time and thought this role would be an insult to his legacy with the team. Wayne's contract ended once the shooting on the film was complete and Cohn would not re-sign him.

With the help of Wayne's agent, Al Kingston of the Leo Morrison Agency, Wayne's unemployment was short lived. Kingston negotiated an offer with Warner Brothers Studios for Wayne to appear in six movies, five of which were Westerns. The nonexclusive contract with the studio not only paid him $1,500 a film but gave him the chance to work elsewhere when opportunities arose.

Kingston took full advantage of the opportunity and bro-kered a second deal with a struggling film company called

Mascot Pictures, the studio responsible for a successful serial starring a dog named Rin-Tin-Tin. Nat Levine, the company's owner, believed he could duplicate the success with a number of action-packed movies featuring a human hero.

Levine offered Wayne $100 a week to play a stunt pilot, a railroad worker, and a member of the French Foreign Legion in three adventure films entitled *Shadow of the Eagle*, *The Hurricane Express*, and *The Three Musketeers*. Levine's serials were small-budget pictures that had a large following and generated a substantial amount of money for the company. Very little time was devoted to filming and generally only one set was used for all interior shots. It was a rewarding and educational experience for Wayne. "We didn't worry about nuances in these serials or B pictures," Wayne told a reporter for *Life* magazine in 1961. "Get the scene on film and get on to the next scene. They were rotten pictures, most of them. But they taught me three things. How to work. How to take orders, and how to get on with the action."

Wayne didn't limit himself to acting or filmmaking. He ventured further into stunt work as well. His mentor in that area was one of Hollywood's finest stuntmen, Yakima Canutt, a rodeo champion turned actor whose exploits as a stuntman were legendary. He was known for his amazing leaps from and onto horses and wagons.

Yakima Canutt and Wayne met on the set of *Shadow of the Eagle*, where Canutt doubled for Wayne on a dangerous motorcycle stunt. Wayne admired Canutt's agility and fearlessness, and Canutt respected Wayne's willingness to learn the craft and attempt to do his own stunts. Under Canutt's watchful eye, Wayne mastered spectacular action sequences and was soon doubling for his stunt mentor.

Canutt played the heavy in several Mascot pictures including many of the films starring Wayne. The two worked together to create a technique that made on-screen fight scenes more realistic. Prior to their effort, when movie characters fought on film, punches were delivered to the shoulders. Wayne and Canutt thought it looked fake and made changes. They found if they stood at a certain angle in front of the camera, they could throw a punch at an actor's face and make it look as if actual contact had been made.

Canutt was proud of his protégé and often bragged about his talent to directors and costars. "Wayne could do a better fight scene than many of the stuntmen working," Canutt once said. "John and I were so competitive and eager to top whatever stunt or fight scene we'd done before that I always thought we could have both been in real danger if we weren't good friends."

In a white hat or a black one, John Wayne's public image as a cowboy was growing. *(Courtesy of the Academy of Motion Picture Arts and Sciences)*

After Wayne completed filming the last of the Mascot serials he was hired to star in another film for Warner Brothers entitled *The Telegraph Trail*. Wayne portrayed an army scout who volunteers to complete the stringing of the telegraph lines across the plains. Canutt played the villain, a vengeful man who led a band of Indians to revolt. He followed the "shoot 'em up" picture with *Somewhere in Sonora*, *Ride 'Em Cowboy*, *The Big Stampede* and *Haunted Gold*.

All of the Warner Brothers' Westerns Wayne was contracted to do were remakes of the films that silent screen star Ken Maynard made in the mid-1920s. In an effort to keep production costs down, many of the original action sequences from Maynard's movies were used in the remakes. Wayne was required to duplicate Maynard's dress and mannerism so the footage would blend.

Wayne's time at Warner Brothers was not solely devoted to the Western genre. Studio executives used the actor, whom they had deemed "quite likeable," in other films as well. He had minor roles in four movies starring such well-known thespians as Douglas Fairbanks Jr., Barbara Stanwyck, and Paul Fix. Fix was a versatile character actor who had appeared in several Westerns. He and Wayne became good friends, and he was also Wayne's unofficial drama coach.

Between Fix's acting advice and Canutt's stunt training, Wayne was able to transform his raw talent into a worthy commodity. However, it was not enough to win over the top brass at Warner Brothers. In the spring of 1933, they decided that Wayne was unable to generate the profits they'd hoped for, and he was dismissed.

Al Kingston immediately secured a position for Wayne at a newly formed motion-picture studio called Republic. Businessman Herbert Yates, who owned Consolidated Films Laboratories, the biggest processor of films in Hollywood, had founded the company earlier that same year. Yates had used his considerable holdings to purchase several small movie studios like Monogram, Majestic Pictures, Liberty Films, and Mascot Films. His goal was to be the largest producer of B Western serials. Yates believed Wayne could help make his dream a reality.

Western musicals were popular with movie-going audiences at the time, and Yates wanted a piece of the business. So, John Wayne was signed to play cowboy crooner and Secret Service agent Singing Sandy Saunders. In a series of sixteen programs, Wayne pretended to strum a guitar and serenade those around him while fighting vicious outlaws. The budget for the films was a meager $10,000. Critics boasted the only redeeming aspect of the productions was Yakima Canutt's stunt work. The films were an embarrassment to Wayne, who felt they made him "look like a pansy." Wayne left Singing Sandy behind once the series was finished.

SW-4

"Strong, silent type" defined John Wayne's early movie personas. (Courtesy of the Academy of Motion Picture Arts and Sciences)

It had become clear to Wayne and those who had a vested interest in his career, that Western pictures were his forte. Republic executives agreed, and although Yates still believed Western musicals could be profitable, he concurred that Wayne was not the right man for the job. Two other actors in his stable of talent, Gene Autry and Roy Rogers, would be the ones to make the studio a fortune riding the range while singing.

Yates gave John Wayne a chance to prove his worth by starring him in a feature entitled *Westward Ho*. He portrayed a wronged son searching for his parents' murderers. The film contained a generous amount of music, but Wayne did not warble a note. The singing was left to his costars: members of the group of men he led called "The Singing Riders." Wayne and his riders fought bandits in saloons and Indians on the open range.

Not only was he convincing as a tough vigilante, but the gentle side he showed opposite the movie's love interest was equally satisfying to fans. Wayne's talent for playing the tempestuous cowhand with a softer side made him appealing to women as well as men. He wasn't afraid his image would be tarnished or that he would lose fans if he kissed the girl.

In 1965 Wayne told a reporter for *Movie Stars Parade Magazine* that he had "made up his mind that he was going to play a real man to the best of his ability." "I feel many of the western stars of the 1920s and '30s were too perfect," he went on to say. "They never drank nor smoked. They never wanted

In *The Man from Monterey* John Wayne continued his string of starring appearances in classic B Westerns. *(Courtesy of the Author)*

to go to bed with a beautiful girl. They never had a fight. . . . They were too sweet and pure. . . . I was trying to play a man who gets dirty, who sweats sometimes, who enjoys really kissing a gal he likes."

Westward Ho was Wayne's twenty-second Western. Many of his peers considered him to be a seasoned veteran of cowboy pictures, but he saw himself as a student of low-budget films. Wayne admitted to colleagues that working on Westerns helped him learn how to talk and speak lines. He learned how to deliver long stretches of dialogue without sounding bored and how to rely on image and action to convey the story.

Wayne was not satisfied with simply learning about how to be a quality actor. He strived to gain all the knowledge he could about the motion picture business, from the financing to production. He had every intention of someday branching out into other areas of filmmaking.

The Dawn Rider was Wayne's follow-up picture to *Westward Ho.* Once again fans could see him chasing after outlaws that killed his family. He was teamed with Yakima Canutt, and the two matched each other evenly in on-screen stunts. Canutt would playfully boast to friends and coworkers on the set that he taught Wayne everything he knew.

Throughout his career Wayne would glean knowledge from a host of talented individuals connected to the industry. The genuine cowboys who worked as extras were the teachers he appreciated the most, however. He respected them and listened eagerly to every story they told about their trail days—absorbing their culture and way of life. Canutt maintained that Wayne's attention to the true wrangler's style made his onscreen portrayal of cowboys realistic and ultimately helped solidify his place in motion-picture history.

———————

"*STAGECOACH* WAS A MILESTONE IN FILM HISTORY AS WELL AS IN JOHN WAYNE'S HISTORY. IT TOOK MY FATHER OUT OF B MOVIES AND PUT HIM INTO CLASS A MOVIES. INTERESTINGLY, IT DID THE SAME THING FOR WESTERNS AS A FILM GENRE."

— *Michael Wayne, John Wayne's son*

STAGECOACH

A brilliant sunset fills the sky behind the sky mesas of
Monument Valley. The desert floor is awash in a soft
light. A team of horses pulling a stagecoach invades the peaceful setting, leaving a cloud of dust in its wake. A pair of drivers
steers the horses along a rugged path up a steep slope toward a
stand of Joshua trees. The passengers inside the stage glance out
the window at the bumpy terrain before them.

Suddenly a rifle blast fires nearby. One of the drivers pulls
wildly on the reins to bring the spooked horses to a stop. They
whinny and buck. The other driver jerks up the shotgun sitting
next to him and holds it close. As the stage reaches the top of
the incline a tall cowboy with deep, blue eyes stands in the
middle of the trail. He wears a faded shirt and trousers and a
hat big enough to shelter a circus. He has a rifle in one hand
and a saddle in the other. The desert stretches out forever in
the distance behind him.

The stage drivers and passengers fix their gaze on the stranger. It's John Wayne as the outlaw Ringo Kid in the film *Stagecoach*. This riveting scene is one of the most memorable introductions of a character in motion-picture history. Wayne's larger-than-life persona dominated the screen, dwarfing the grand Arizona landscape and overshadowing performances by a handful of Hollywood's most compelling actors.

———————

John Wayne was thirty-one years old and a veteran of more than sixty films when he made *Stagecoach*. He had twirled six-shooters, tossed rope, busted broncos, and foiled cattle rustlers in B Westerns for five different studios. He was a battle-scarred graduate of the sagebrush school of screen drama, but he was still not as well known as stars like Gene Autry and Roy Rogers, who had fewer films behind them. The 1939 release of *Stagecoach*, directed by John Ford and starring Thomas Mitchell, Claire Trevor, and John Carradine, brought Wayne into the limelight.

After five years of being ignored by his one-time mentor John Ford, Wayne received a message from the unpredictable director inviting him to meet him on his yacht, which was anchored in Long Beach harbor. Wayne couldn't help but wonder why he was being summoned and was surprised when Ford greeted the actor as though no time had passed since they last spoke. He invited Wayne to join him and his other guests—all familiar faces to Wayne. Actors Johnny Weismuller and Ward

Bond, and screenwriter Dudley Nichols were among those invited to stay.

Ford was personable, the dinner conversation was scintillating, and the ship's bar was well stocked. The men played cards and talked about fishing, but no mention was made about why Ford had never returned the calls Wayne had made to him over the years and no apology was offered for his unjustified actions. Wayne accepted that Ford's devotion could be temporal and was willing to give the director the benefit of the doubt.

That first meeting in the summer of 1935 grew into a weekly reunion for Wayne and his friends. "The Young Men's Purity Total Abstinence and Snooker Pool Association," as they referred to themselves, spent numerous weekends aboard Ford's boat the *Araner*. Lifelong friendships were formed and a fair amount of alcohol was consumed. Wayne, as well as the other actors in the association, sought Ford's advice on their careers. Ford reviewed Wayne's studio contracts and offered suggestions on script selection but would not extend himself beyond that.

When Wayne wasn't with Ford and the other members of the association, he visited with his father, Clyde. The two spent many weekends together watching Wayne's brother Robert play professional football for the Los Angeles Dons. Clyde was proud of his sons and looked forward to watching their success continue. His health was on the decline, however. On March 4, 1937, Clyde Morrison passed away in his sleep. A massive heart attack had claimed his life. John Wayne was devastated.

Co-starring with the beautiful Claire Trevor in *Stagecoach*, John Wayne moved out of B Westerns into a career as an "A-list" star. *(Courtesy of the Academy of Motion Picture Arts and Sciences)*

Wayne's friends and family helped see him through the heartbreaking ordeal. But more hard times were on the way. By mid-1937, not only had he lost his father but his work as a cowboy actor had slowed to a stop. Although two years had passed since his reconciliation with John Ford, they had still not worked on a movie together. Then Ford asked Wayne to read the screenplay for *Stagecoach*.

Based on a short story entitled *Stage to Lordsburg* by Ernest Hayox, *Stagecoach* was the story of a hazardous journey of an odd assortment of frontier characters making their way through the Indian territory in New Mexico. Ford purchased the rights to the tale for $4,000. After it was turned into a screenplay, he made the rounds to studios looking for money to produce the picture. Most Hollywood executives turned him down and gave as their reason that "Westerns don't sell." Ford spent the better part of 1937 searching for a financial backer before producer Walter Wanger finally agreed to fund the film and gave John Ford a total budget of $546,000 to make the movie.

Initially, both Ford and Wagner had wanted Gary Cooper to play the part of the Ringo Kid, but the limited budget kept Ford from hiring the high-priced actor. Wayne was Ford's second choice for the role, but he was convinced he could get a quality performance from the celluloid cowboy. Since making *The Big Trail* he believed the young actor had developed the skills and personality necessary to be in a major motion picture.

Wayne was flattered that Ford considered him at all and eagerly consented to joining the cast of *Stagecoach*. He was the least-paid actor on the film, earning a modest $3,000 for the job. Wayne was willing to accept the nominal fee for the chance to work with his idol again. He not only felt a sense of obligation to Ford for giving him his first on-camera job but also saw him as a second father. Friends and industry professionals aware of Wayne's allegiance to the director believed Ford took advantage of Duke. Wayne disagreed. "It's an honor to work for him. He can be a real son-of-a-bitch," Duke admitted in an interview for *American Weekly Magazine* in 1954, "but he ultimately wanted the best for me and by God he always got it."

Principal photography for *Stagecoach* began on October 31, 1938. Ford surveyed the cast at the first reading of the script like a king overseeing his minions. He puffed on his pipe while listening to their delivery, making suggestions and changes to the dialogue when necessary. Ford rehearsed alone with Wayne and had him repeat his lines over and over again until he felt Duke had the right timing and infliction he required. The cameras were turned on once Ford was satisfied with the rehearsals.

Ford was methodical, deliberate, and frequently unkind. Actor Paul Fix believed the way Ford treated the people that worked for him was "degrading to their spirit." No one was exempt from Ford's gruff, militaristic style of directing, least of all John Wayne.

John Wayne and stuntman Yakima Canutt developed realistic and thrilling stunts for the movie *Stagecoach*. *(Courtesy of the Academy of Motion Picture Arts and Sciences)*

Ford's open criticism of Wayne during the shooting of the film was difficult for the other cast members to witness. He blasted the actor's speech, mannerisms, and the way he walked. In an interview with Randy Roberts, Claire Trevor, the actress who played Dallas in *Stagecoach*, stated that Ford was "determined to make Wayne into his idea of an actor and wasn't gentle about it." She recalled him grabbing Wayne by the chin and shaking him. "Why are you moving your mouth so much?" Ford would bark. "Don't you know that you don't act with your mouth in pictures? You act with your eyes!" Trevor added that "it was tough for Duke to take, but he took it."

Ford's harsh treatment of Wayne was interrupted once by actor Tim Holt. He suggested the director "lay off the poor guy." It was exactly what the other cast and crew members were thinking but didn't dare say. Ford eased up, but only for a short time.

Wayne himself challenged the notion that Ford loved to be cruel to his actors. He maintained that the director was harsh because he wanted a quality of performance. "Mr. Ford only wanted to do one thing," Wayne told reporters for *Movie Magazine* in 1956, "and that was make good pictures. To achieve that he would do anything, anything." Wayne also noted that because Ford treated him like an outcast on the set and during the filming, it made his portrayal of the outcast Ringo Kid all the more believable.

Stagecoach was released in March 1939. The film received glowing reviews, and critics singled out Wayne's performance, praising him for his fine and memorable work. Not only were his acting skills recognized, reviewers applauded his stunt work as well. Wayne and Canutt did the majority of the picture's stunts, and B. Franks of *Movie Star Parade Magazine* called their efforts "ground breaking." "The *Stagecoach* stunts are unsurpassed and have the beauty and precision of a ballet filled with danger," Franks concluded.

Movie-going audiences shared the critics' high regard for the film and the Motion Picture Academy echoed the sentiment. The picture was nominated for seven Oscars, including best director and best supporting actor. Wayne was not nominated for an Academy Award, but the compliment he received from Ford for his work in the film was satisfaction enough. "He knew his lines, and he did what he was told to do," Ford told a reporter for *Life* magazine in 1958. "Of course I surrounded him with superb actors, and some of that glitter rubbed off on his shoulders. But he's still up there with the best of them. He's damn good."

Stagecoach lifted Wayne out of B Western films and helped elevate Westerns as a whole. But Wayne still did not fully realize how much excitement his role as the Ringo Kid was causing in film circles. His peers and film executives felt he was every bit as good as another talented actor who got his start riding horses, Gary Cooper.

Herbert Yates, president of Republic Studios, capitalized on the star status Wayne achieved from Ford's films. Yates had loaned the actor out to Wagner Productions to make *Stagecoach* but refused to let Wayne appear in any other project outside of Republic until his contract was fulfilled. Wayne made five more movies for Republic,

TALKIES

Stagecoach If you liked the "Covered Wagon" you'll cheer this. Nine people set out through hostile Apache country—nine people of vastly different characters. Then the story develops their characters skillfully, while the stagecoach gets into one of the best-sustained and most exciting frontier fight scenes you ever saw. The photography is spectacular, and makes

Lots of excitement in top-of-the-month film "Stagecoach"

you proud to be a citizen of a great democracy that has such vistas. *George Bancroft, John Wayne, Louise Platt* and a big gang. Top of the month by head and shoulders.

This review of *Stagecoach* appeared in *Farm Journal* in April 1939. *(Courtesy* Farm Journal, Inc.*)*

low-budget Westerns in which he received third and fourth billing. Each picture was a success, and Hollywood filmmakers were becoming convinced that Wayne was the reason.

When his time at Republic was up, Wayne was offered a part in *The Long Voyage Home*. Swapping his rifle and coonskin cap for a marlin spike, Wayne portrayed Ollie, the inarticulate, Swedish sailor in Eugene O'Neill's classic tale. John Ford would once again direct Wayne's performance.

Wayne's slow, easy-going shyness, his lack of pretense, and his naturalness were traits that made him well liked on and off the screen. Regardless of his popularity, his friends and colleagues noted that Wayne never saw himself as a potential star. In an article authored by celebrity reporter Gene Schrolt for *Motion Picture Magazine*, Schrolt wrote that "while everyone is already beginning to treat him with the respect reserved for the top notchers, he goes along simply and unaffected by it all."

Wayne's unwillingness to believe that he was slated for stardom may have been due in part to his previous experience with *The Big Trail*. He had anticipated career advancement that point. The fact that it didn't materialize left Wayne thinking his career would end where it began, in the saddle. Hollywood had other plans. After being overlooked for ten years and relegated to an almost forgotten place in Westerns, the spotlight suddenly turned full force upon him.

Over the course of his fifty-year career, Wayne was often asked the difference between his early body of work and other cowboy actors of the same era. Wayne's answer was consistent. "The only thing that set me apart from my fellow range riders," Duke confessed, "was John Ford."

"I COULDN'T IMAGINE BEING THE CHILD
OF ANYBODY ELSE. HE WAS A GREAT
DAD AND A GREAT FRIEND AND GAVE
ME INCREDIBLE OPPORTUNITIES."

— *Patrick Wayne, John Wayne's son*

MARRIED
WITH
CHILDREN

Gunslinger Quirt Evans, as portrayed by John Wayne in *Angel and the Badman*, sauntered out of a log cabin situated in picturesque Monument Valley and headed toward his restless horse. He was limping slightly—the result of a bullet wound in his leg. The injury had temporarily forced him to abandon his search for the outlaws who killed his father. Now that he was on the mend, he would be on his way.

Before he reached his mustang, he heard a voice calling after him. He turned to see beautiful Penelope Worth, the Quaker woman who nursed him back to health. The two stared longingly into one another's eyes. The innocent lady had fallen in love with the scoundrel and was offering to go with him. Wayne's character felt too much for her to allow her to join him on his vendetta, but at the same time he couldn't bear to leave her behind. The bad man decided to stay with the angel. The romantic gesture was rewarded with a happy, tearful sigh of relief from his co-star.

————

John Wayne not only charmed co-stars but captivated female audiences as well. However, young Duke only had eyes for the elegant Beverly Hills debutante Josephine Saenz.

Early in his career Duke Morrison was uncomfortable with the attention he received from lady admirers, but he was not unaccustomed to it. As a handsome football player for the University of Southern California, he had an active social life. But until he was introduced to the gorgeous and demure Josephine Saenz in 1926, no one had completely captured his interest.

Duke met Josephine at a Thanksgiving dance that his college fraternity was hosting. He and his escort for the evening had double-dated with another couple that had included Josephine. The two were instantly smitten and by the end of the evening were making plans to see each other again.

Josephine's background was unlike Duke's in almost every way. Her family was directly descended from Spanish royalty and was counted among Southern California's elite. Her father was a prominent businessman and her mother was a genteel French lady who doted on her children and raised her daughters to be prim and proper. Both her mother and her father were devoted Catholics who were very involved in the church.

Duke was awestruck by Josephine's poise and kind manner. He was awkward and tongue-tied around her. Josephine found the modest athlete engaging. In an interview he gave to biographer Maurice Zolotow in 1967, Duke described the overwhelming feelings he initially had for Josephine. "I was so hypnotized I don't think I said more than two words on our first date. I remember opening the door of the car for her, and my fingers happened to graze her arm as she was standing on the running board, kind of pulling this black coat around her. A shiver went through me. I knew it must be love."

In a short time Josephine and Duke felt deeply enough about one another that the subject of marriage naturally followed. Mr. and Mrs. Saenz strenuously objected to the match and made their feelings known. Duke assured Josephine's parents that his heart for their daughter was true, but his sincerity was not the issue. Duke was an unemployed teenager with no social standing, money, or prospects. A part-time actor who did not regularly attend church was not the sort of man the Saenzes wanted Josephine to commit herself to. She was forbidden to see him.

For awhile the pair secretly defied Josephine's parents. They refused to break off their engagement and decided to keep it a secret. Duke pursued a more steady position at Fox studios and ultimately secured a job that paid him $40 a week. It was a salary he felt would support him and Josephine. She applauded his efforts but could not be persuaded to marry without her parents' consent. Duke was hurt and angry. The two abruptly parted ways, with Duke saying things he would later regret.

His heart was broken and his pride was beaten down when he chose to leave Los Angeles. In an attempt to rid himself of the pain and disappointment he was feeling, he fled to San Francisco. Josephine's decision not to marry him was not the only reason he wanted to get away. His college career had also come to a sudden end when a shoulder injury had sidelined him as a football player, which ultimately cost him his scholarship and his chance to finish school.

Once he reached San Francisco he tried to find work, and when that proved unsuccessful he snuck aboard a steamship bound for Hawaii called the SS *Malolo*. He hoped the sea would help him forget his hardships. Less than a day into the journey, Duke Morrison found the exercise to have had the exact opposite effect. The beautiful woman he'd left behind was all he could think about.

Duke had been woefully lacking in funds when he conceived the idea of sailing off into the blue. Unable to afford passage on the cruise ship, he decided to stow away. For three days and nights he strolled in and out of the common areas undetected. Finding something to eat and a place to sleep kept him busy, but Josephine occupied the bulk of his thoughts. Her memory did not stay behind as he had hoped. During his travels he realized how much he still loved her and wanted to be with her.

The dilemma over what to do about the flood of emotions assaulting Duke was quickly remedied when the ship's crew discovered he was a stowaway. Duke was arrested and locked in a windowless room below deck. He would be handed over to the authorities when the vessel returned to San Francisco. One of Wayne's friends at Fox studios helped persuade the cruise-ship line not to press charges against him and also provided him with a train ticket home.

On May 23, 1927, Duke returned to Los Angeles and to Josephine. He hurried to her house and professed his love. During his absence Josephine had been very ill, but when she saw Duke her health began to improve. Josephine's mother noticed the change in her daughter's disposition and acknowledged that Duke was the reason. The Saenzes reconsidered the couple's desire to be together and agreed that after a proper betrothal period, they could marry.

On June 24, 1933, after a six-year engagement, Marion (Duke) Morrison and Josephine Saenz were wed. The couple exchanged vows in a lavish ceremony held at a spectacular estate in Bel Air, and among the guests were actors Loretta Young and George O'Brien. Wayne's parents and brother attended the event as well. Wayne was nervous that Molly would create a scene on his wedding day because she didn't want his father to be at the ceremony, but she was cordial to her ex-husband and the bride. Later in the evening at the reception, Molly admitted to family friends that she thought

Duke and Josie were wrong for each other and that the marriage wouldn't last. She felt the fire had died out of her son and daughter-in-law's relationship by the time they wed. As it turned out, Molly was right on both accounts.

Wayne did not settle easily into married life. He spent a great deal of time away from home working and furthering his acting career. During his absence Josephine transformed the three-room apartment they called home into a stylish, picture-perfect showplace. She organized and hosted dinner parties and charitable events and always invited church leaders, nuns, and priests from the local parish to join them. Duke was not a socialite and the posh affairs his new wife arranged made him feel uncomfortable. Josephine insisted that such events were essential for creating a respectable reputation for the future of the children they would eventually have. Wayne disagreed but never stood in the way of Josephine's participation in any social, religious, or benevolent activities.

As time went on Wayne found excuses to remove himself from high society. He preferred a more simple life. For her part, Josephine had never been enamored with the Hollywood scene and distanced herself from that part of Wayne's life as much as possible. Their opposing viewpoints took a toll on the marriage.

The happiest times the couple shared were with their four children. Michael was born on November 23, 1934, Mary on February 26, 1936, Patrick on July 15, 1939, and Melinda on December 3, 1940. While Wayne's family occasionally accompanied him to various locations where he would be shooting a motion picture, Josephine was not fond of following her husband from place to place. She and the children would be holed up in a hotel room while Wayne worked twelve- and fourteen-hour days. She let Wayne know that she was unhappy, and that added to his growing his resentment toward her.

Josephine absorbed herself in the life she was accustomed to, and Duke immersed himself in his. When Wayne wasn't making films, he was spending time with his friends at the Hollywood Athletic Club or aboard Ford's boat, the *Araner*. He preferred unassuming company where he was free to drink, fish, and hunt over the reserved and restrictive home life with Josephine. In the process, he neglected his sons and daughters. Wayne was not unaware of that fact, and in 1936 he made an attempt to be a traditional type of father and husband. He gave up acting and pursued jobs with schedules that left his evenings free to be with his family, working at a variety of non-film industry jobs such as real estate and prize fighting. After six months, however, his acting coach, Paul Fix, lured him back into show business.

By 1938 Duke and Josephine's marriage was nearing an end. Years after the pair had gone their separate ways, Wayne admitted to his friend Ward Bond that he and Josephine should have separated right away. "But I was in love with her," he said, "and when the children came, we both wanted to work it out." Duke made a sincere effort to change for Josephine and to reconcile with her. He didn't want his children to be exposed to the same bitterness and resentment that he had lived with as a boy, watching his parents' marriage disintegrate. "We held out as long as we could," Wayne told Ward Bond.

Although Josephine knew her marriage was over, as a staunch Catholic she could not be persuaded to file for divorce. The church would not sanction such an act. The Waynes decided to make the most of a difficult situation and to endure for their children's sake. Years passed and the gulf between the two continued to widen.

From 1938 to 1941, the couple maintained a civil, respectable relationship. She cared for their family and he provided for them with a generous income. For a time it seemed the unusual marriage might go on indefinitely, and then Wayne met a sultry Latin actress named Esperanza Baur Diaz Ceballos, called Chata.

Shortly after he was introduced to Chata, the two began a torrid love affair. Wayne's friends cautioned him not to let his infatuation get out of control. John Ford tried to steer his attention back toward Josephine and his children, but his advice was not well received. Wayne resented any interference in his personal life.

News of Chata and Wayne's liaison soon reached Josephine, but for a time she held out hope that she and Duke would reconcile. By October 1943, however, Wayne's relationship with Chata was stronger than ever. Josephine relented and filed for divorce. The settlement was final on November 1, 1944.

Gossip columnists from coast to coast gleefully sought interviews with friends close to the Wayne family, and Hollywood
magazines reported on the sordid details of the divorce proceedings. Even one of the nation's leading newspapers could not
resist publicizing the proceedings.

John Wayne, actor, yesterday was sued for divorce under his true
name of Marion M. Morrison by his wife, Mrs. Josephine S.
Morrison, society figure, who charged extreme cruelty.

Mrs. Morrison said in her complaint that the couple has entered
into a property settlement and an agreement regarding support and
custody of their four children, Michael Anthony, 9; Mary Antonia,
8; Patrick John, 5; and Melinda Ann Morrison, 3.

No details of the property settlement, or custody agreement
were mentioned.

Mrs. Morrison charged the film actor with "repeated acts of cruel
and inhuman treatment" which caused her "physical and mental
suffering." The complaint was filed by Attorney George M. Breslin.

Breslin released a statement in her behalf in which she stated
that "because of my religion, I regarded divorce as a purely civil
action in no way affecting the moral status of marriage," but said
she had received permission from the proper church authority to
ask for the divorce which she believed "the only available means of
clarifying the position of my children."

Los Angeles Times—November 1, 1944

Josephine took the divorce hard. Her nearly ten-year marriage had ended in scandal and she was embarrassed and angry.

Once the legal matters were finalized, Josephine refused to speak with Wayne about the children or allow him to pick them up for his weekly visits. A family friend transported the children back and forth between their parents' homes.

In time Josephine's bitterness faded and she and Duke were civil again. Wayne always referred to his ex-wife as a "wonderful mother" and was grateful to her for not making the children hate him. "I'm thankful for that," Wayne admitted in an interview with biographer Maurice Zolotow. "Because of Josephine's example and attitude I believe I got along better with my children and saw more of them after we were divorced."

Throughout the course of his career, Wayne's personal life was the subject of many articles and exposes. In 1952, Wayne appeared on the cover of *Time* magazine. For the accompanying Josephine was asked to comment on her ex-husband and expound on her time with the legendary cowboy. "Success and the complications that went along with it robbed Duke of the simplicity he found good," Josephine stated. "Before *Stagecoach*, he was a serenely happy husband."

Wayne did not disagree with that statement. In retrospect he believed he had never been as content as he was with Josephine. "I didn't see it then," he confessed to his friend Paul Fix in 1960, "but my divorce from Josie was the stupidest thing I ever did in my life. She was a woman whose weaknesses were outweighed by her strengths."

Three weeks after Wayne's divorce was final, he married Chata Bauer. The marriage proved to be one of Wayne's more regrettable actions. But, by the time his first marriage had dissolved, Duke's film career was in high gear. He no longer sought solace from life's disappointments sneaking aboard cruise ships; instead he soldiered through the heartaches making movies.

Motion pictures were a great comfort for Wayne. "Guts made him an actor," assistant director Joseph Kane said in 1954. "Duke made Westerns what they are today and those movies got him over any rough personal spots, making him a star in the process."

————

"HIS IMAGE HAD AS MUCH IMPACT IN THE WORLD. . . . DUKE WAS A GREAT ACTOR, A GREAT HUMANITARIAN, BUT ALWAYS HIMSELF."

— *Actress Elizabeth Taylor*

A REEL
COWBOY

High above the rocky terrain a mat of black, rainless clouds moved steadily across the sky. Under this overcast a wind from the north blew tirelessly. In the near distance multiple hoof beats could be heard fast approaching, the quick rhythm blending with the sound of dust devils swirling about. Suddenly, a wagon train led by a frantic team of six horses plows through the setting. The driver of the vehicle steered the animals around jagged rocks and mounds of dirt. The pop-eyed passengers aboard the prairie schooner were tossed about like rag dolls. A regiment of guerilla soldiers rode with a fury after the vehicle.

The wagon's capable pilot was John Wayne. In the most daring sequence in the 1940 motion picture *Dark Command*, Wayne and stunt coordinator Yakima Canutt hurried the horses to the edge of a cliff and brought the animals to an abrupt stop. An angry mob of extras clad in Confederate uniforms bore down fast behind them. The cowboy actors sized up the dilemma and in an instant jerked tightly on the reins and spurred the team of horses over the rough crag into the raging water. It was a spectacular stunt.

———————

When *Dark Command* was released, the attention the film received was due, in large part, to John Wayne. Since appearing as the Ringo Kid in *Stagecoach*, his popularity had soared, but the film's amazing stunts were another attraction. Wayne and Canutt orchestrated the dive off the cliff, using a giant trough to achieve the amazing action sequence. Several stuntmen, along with the wagon and the horses, slid down a 40-foot chute and plummeted into a wash along with the wagon and horses.

No stunt actors were injured in the execution of the dangerous feat, but two of the animals died as a result of the fall. The stunt not only attracted audiences but drew criticism from the American Society for the Prevention of Cruelty to Animals. The death of the horses prompted changes to be made in the handling of animals while filming motion pictures. Publicity surrounding the incident also brought more people out to see the movie. The film grossed an unprecedented $3 million and further solidified Wayne's place as a rising box-office commodity.

John Ford's 1939 classic *Stagecoach* had made John Wayne a star, but Wayne was still under contract at Republic when recognition for his abilities finally arrived. And while Herbert Yates was more than willing to capitalize on the actor's notoriety, he had not been willing to gamble the studio's money on bigger budget films that showcased Wayne's talents. For four years Yates used Wayne almost exclusively in B Westerns. He occasionally loaned the actor out to other Hollywood studios interested in developing Wayne's talent, but Yates risked nothing on Duke.

Dark Command cost $750,000 to make. It was Republic's most expensive and ambitious film to date, earning Wayne a reported $5,500 for playing the part of Kansas Sheriff Bob Seton. As in *Stagecoach*, he was paired with Claire Trevor. Audiences liked their on-screen chemistry. Yates would take advantage of that as well.

Rauol Walsh, the director who had hired Wayne to star in *The Big Trail*, directed *Dark Command*. Walsh was impressed with how Wayne's acting style had matured since their last picture together and was anxious to work with him again. In Walsh's autobiography, *Each Man in His Time*, he noted that one of the proudest accomplishments in his career was the discovering of John Wayne. "He's a gifted actor with incredible range," Walsh wrote. "He's the quintessential cowboy hero both on and off screen."

Wayne's performance in *Dark Command* proved that the job he did in *Stagecoach* was not simply a fluke. Film critics boasted that Wayne "impressively carried off one of his best roles." *Daily Variety* hailed the movie as a success and noted that "the film established the fact that Westerns can be A films" and that "John Wayne was the champion of the genre."

After more than ten years in the movie business, Wayne was finally getting respect. With that respect came the privilege of being more selective about the roles he choose to accept. Some of Hollywood's most popular directors such as David Selznik, Victor Fleming, and Mervyn LeRoy, took notice of Wayne's talent and invited him to meet with them and discuss the possibility of working together.

Shortly before the release of *Dark Command* in 1940, Cecil B. DeMille began courting Wayne in order to persuade him to join the cast of a motion picture entitled *Reap the Wild Wind*.

Wayne had previously met DeMille in 1937, when DeMille had asked him to his office to discuss the possibility of him appearing in a Western he was producing called *The Plainsman*. Wayne made the appointment, but was kept waiting more than an hour before DeMille would see him. During that meeting DeMille critiqued Wayne's body of work and explained why he would not be casting him in the film.

Reap the Wild Wind featured John Wayne as the captain of a salvage ship off the Florida Keys. *(Courtesy of the Academy of Motion Picture Arts and Sciences)*

When DeMille approached him about *Reap the Wild Wind*, Wayne had not forgotten the director's behavior of three years earlier and did not agree to meet with him. DeMille persisted, sending a letter of admiration to Wayne and a copy of *Reap the Wild Wind* for him to review. Wayne did read the script and responded with a seventeen-page list of suggested changes. DeMille called the actor and thanked him for his input and told him how much he needed John Wayne in the picture. It took several meetings before Wayne changed his mind about the film and its director, but he eventually agreed to appear opposite Ray Milland and Paulette Goddard.

A newspaper ad for *Reap the Wild Wind* that appeared in a Midwest newspaper in 1942. *(Courtesy of the Academy of Motion Picture Arts and Sciences)*

While waiting for production to begin on *Reap the Wild Wind*, Wayne fulfilled his contract with Republic Pictures. He appeared in two Westerns, one with Betty Field and another with Marlene Dietrich, and then a War Epic with Joan Crawford. Wayne received favorable reviews for each of his performances and *Daily Variety* reported what Herbert Yates already knew: "John Wayne is a valuable piece of property."

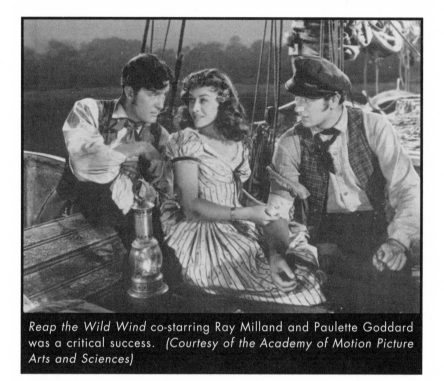

Reap the Wild Wind co-starring Ray Milland and Paulette Goddard was a critical success. *(Courtesy of the Academy of Motion Picture Arts and Sciences)*

Reap the Wild Wind opened on March 19, 1942. The grand melodrama featured Wayne as the captain of a salvage ship in Key West, Florida. Fierce ocean storms and giant sea creatures stood in the way of Wayne doing his job and rescuing the woman he loved from pirates. The movie earned an Academy Award for visual effects. Wayne received glowing praise for his performance from his fans, from his peers, and from DeMille himself.

Reap the Wild Wind was one of seven pictures starring Wayne released in 1942. After the success of *Dark Command*, Yates had wasted no time setting up production on a variety of Republic-backed films, casting his number-one-money-making star in the lead. Wayne returned to the Western genre in the films *Lady for a Night* and *In Old California*. Yates teamed Wayne and Marlene Dietrich again in the movie *Pittsburgh*. The on-screen passion between the sultry, German actress and the larger-than-life cowboy sold tickets. One of the reasons the act was so convincing was that the pair was involved off screen as well.

Throughout the course of his early career, Wayne was linked romantically to a number of Hollywood starlets including Sigrid Gurie, Paulette Goddard, and Clair Trevor. With the exception of Marlene Dietrich, the rumors of extramarital affairs were just that.

The interest Dietrich and Wayne had for one another was strictly professional in the beginning. But during the filming of their first movie together, *Seven Sinners*, the actress suggested they be more than colleagues. Wayne found in Dietrich someone who would attend industry events with him and discuss the profession. Wayne's first wife, Josephine, had always distanced herself from the motion-picture business, which had a negative impact on their marriage. As a result, Duke was vulnerable to Dietrich's amorous pursuits, and the two eventually became lovers. Their three-year affair ended shortly after *Pittsburgh* was released. Not only had the relationship simply run its course, Dietrich had decided to take a break from making movies to tour Europe and entertain the troops fighting against the Nazis.

In Old California signaled a return to the Western genre for John Wayne. *(Courtesy of the Academy of Motion Picture Arts and Sciences)*

Wayne was inspired by Dietrich's patriotic actions. Many of his fellow thespians were recruited by the Armed Forces and proudly went to do their duty for their country. At thirty-five Duke was not a candidate for the draft, and Republic would not have let him out of his studio contract to enlist. Wayne felt compelled to serve in any way he could, however. A plea from President Franklin D. Roosevelt to the Hollywood community showed Wayne how he could help the war effort.

"The American motion picture," Roosevelt informed the film industry, "is one of the most effective tools for informing and entertaining our citizens." John Wayne was motivated to do his part, helping to create films that promoted American involvement in the war effort and were entertaining in the process.

Herbert Yates was very much aware of Wayne's desire to come to his country's aid, and he also never lost sight of the substantial profit Wayne made the studio. With that in mind, Yates cast Duke in a war picture called *Flying Tigers*. The film was based on the exploits of American flyers in China who battled against the Japanese long before Pearl Harbor. Wayne was perfectly suited for the role as leader of the airborne volunteer group known as the Tigers. The movie was an overwhelming success for Republic.

Motion-picture industry leaders took notice of how Wayne resonated with movie-goers. Patriotic audiences admired him, and directors with war films in the works set their sights on the actor to star. From 1943 to 1945, Wayne alternated between appearing in Westerns and War Epics. In the R.K.O. film *A Lady Takes a Chance*, he portrayed a rodeo rider in love with a beautiful tourist. In the *Fighting Seabees* he played the leader of a group of men building military sites in the Pacific. His next picture called for his return to the frontier as a cowboy framed for murder in *Tall in the Saddle*. Then a call from John Ford led Wayne to one of the most pivotal roles of his career, that of Naval Lieutenant Rusty Ryan in *They Were Expendable*. Critics and fans praised Wayne's performance calling it "the best acting of his career."

9 **Although Woody is dismissed** from the squadron, he learns that Jim (left) plans to bomb a supply train—alone. Woody (right) sneaks into the transport, takes the controls.

10 **When the plane catches fire,** Woody, wounded, pushes Jim out, to parachute to safety. Woody, the mercenary pilot, dives into the train and dies in the flaming plane.

END

Photoplay Magazine carried this advertisement for Republic Studio's wartime drama *Flying Tigers* starring John Wayne and John Carroll. *(Courtesy of* Time *magazine)*

CINEMA

Hollywood at War

Director George Stevens (*The Talk of the Town*) last week rhetorically answered a rhetorical question: "How can the movies best aid the war effort?" The discussion, in which Novelist Erskine Caldwell, Cinemactress Rosalind Russell, Walt Disney and others also joined plangent voices, was broadcast on the American Forum of the Air.

Said Director Stevens: "In these times the only actor that I would like to direct is Sessue Hayakawa. ... Some of you old-time moviegoers remember him. ... Well Sessue, if this gets to you in Tokyo ... here's an offer for you. Slip into the mouse-green uniform of a Jap general and some fine sundown when we get over there we'll take a shot of you climbing up to that high point on the island of Corregidor where the flagpole stands ... and from the top of that shell-scarred mast you'll pull down your meat-ball flag. Then you and the rest of your gang will stand at attention while Douglas MacArthur puts the Stars & Stripes back up there. ... And ... Sessue ... that music you're hearing is our theme, the old *Star-Spangled Banner* ... you remember that ... and when it gets to the 'Oh say can you see' part ... Sessue ... you take off your hat and brush a tear from your eye ... whether you've got one there or not ... because you're sorry ... Sessue ... sorry you're a Jap. Then we fade out.

"That's the kind of movie it would be a real pleasure to make."

New Picture

Flying Tigers (Republic) is an overlong but unpretentious, genuine tribute to those U.S. volunteer airmen who, against some of the toughest odds in the history of aerial warfare, fought the Japs in the air above China before Pearl Harbor.

The story, part pulp dramatics, part pure action, is that hardy perennial about the squadron commander (John Wayne); his friend, the nurse (Anna Lee); the rookie who gets killed (William Shirley); the oldtimer who gets grounded (Paul Kelly); the drunk who is given Another Chance (Edmund MacDonald); the show-off individualist (John Carroll) who learns, at last, what the fight is about, but not until he has played hob with the squadron's morale, matériel and lifeblood. This simple stereotype proves adequate to convey some of the true power and meaning of simple men doing a life-&-death job together, and something, too, of what they are doing it for.

For this success John Wayne and Paul Kelly are chiefly responsible. Kelly, and some of the other members of the squadron, play their parts manfully, for all they are worth. John Wayne is a rudimentary actor, but he has the look and bearing, unusual in his trade, of a capable human male. As the squadron commander, he is able to make his habitual inarticu-

lateness suggest the uncommunicative competence that men expect in their leaders. Anna Lee, after three sleepless nights, is still able to suggest a Beautyrest. Too many Japanese pilots get the same wound, by which they bleed photogenically at the mouth. But when the dragon-headed planes are off the ground, and fighting, *Flying Tigers* is a good show to see. For the combat sequences, salted with some extraordinary shots made

JOHN WAYNE
Violence insured a rosy future.

in Burma, are always loud, swift, exciting. At moments, as in the sudden, braided smoke spirals of two earthward hurtling planes, they are superb.

* * *

Solid (6 ft. 2) John Wayne, 35, found it very easy to get into films, and very slow going, after he got there. Wayne, born Marion Michael Morrison in Winterset, Iowa, was raised on a California ranch. At the University of Southern California he picked up the nickname "Duke," was an honor student. Vacations, he worked as a truck driver, an iceman, a prop man for Fox.

"Duke" was hauling furniture around a set for *Born Reckless* when Director Raoul Walsh spotted him, ordered him for god's sake not to cut his hair, which had grown shaggy at the nape. Then "Duke" was renamed John Wayne, pushed ahead of some 82 other candidates for the juvenile lead in *The Big Trail*. He did very nicely with the part. Later he made a personal-appearance tour on which, to his embarrassment, he was required to keep his hillbilly hair in a rich fringe over his collar.

In 1933 Wayne married Josephine Saenz, daughter of a Panamanian Consul. Otherwise he just worked. He worked in clutching-hand serials, and in some three dozen Westerns. It was not until John Ford

TIME, October 12, 1942

Although John Wayne enjoyed playing heroic parts, he longed to direct and produce his own movies. He had studied Ford's work habits and dedication to a project, and he was determined to follow in his footsteps. His ultimate goal was to form a production company and to bring to the big screen the story of the brave men who fought at the Alamo. Wayne hoped to convince Herbert Yates to give him a chance to accomplish his goal at Republic.

In September 1945, Wayne negotiated a seven-picture deal with Republic Studios. The revised, nonexclusive contract provided him with a guaranteed percentage of the gross profits of his films and the opportunity to produce motion pictures. One of those pictures was to be *The Alamo*. He also signed a five-year contract with R.K.O. Radio Pictures, soon to be owned by his good friend, Howard Hughes.

According to records at the Academy of Motion Picture Arts and Sciences, Herbert Yates only mildly resented giving up the control he had over Wayne for so many years. Duke was still among his stable of contract players, and any Republic film starring the actor made a profit. Profits were always Yates's chief concern and he made whatever concessions needed to be made to ensure them.

By 1949 Wayne had made all but one of the movies promised to Republic under his new agreement with Yates. His dream project, *The Alamo,* would be the seventh picture produced for the studio, but Yates disagreed with Wayne's $3 million

Movie posters and other advertisements for *Flying Tigers* played up its patriotic message. *(Courtesy of the Academy of Motion Picture Arts and Sciences)*

production price tag. The two heatedly debated the issue. Yates insisted on cutting costs, and Duke insisted that doing so would compromise the integrity of the story.

In the end, John Wayne walked out on Yates, refusing to do the film at all with Republic. The action effectively ended Wayne's fifteen-year relationship with the studio. The falling out had an adverse effect on Republic Pictures. Industry professionals who had long believed that Yates was too cheap refused to do business with him. With the decline in the popularity of the B Westerns and Yates's unwillingness to spend the money needed to create a quality product, Republic Pictures stopped making movies.

John Wayne did not.

———————

A STAR'S MAIL

At the height of his career, John Wayne received an average of 18,000 fan letters a month. Wayne's private secretary, Mary St. John, answered many letters for the actor, but he responded to a number of them personally. It was not uncommon for him to answer requests for autographed photos and questions about his work. Oftentimes he would get letters from fans who insisted they attended school together, grew up in the same town, or wanted to share something they believed about his past. Wayne gladly wrote those admirers, correcting any misconceptions they might have about his upbringing. His gracious response to the people who took the time to write him offers unique insight into the early life of the film legend.

JOHN WAYNE

9570 Wilshire Boulevard
Suite 400
Beverly Hills, California 90212
February 5, 1975

Glen A. Settle
Rt. #1-Box 98
Rosamond, California   93560

Dear Mr. Settle:

I was born in 1907 so I would have been seven years old in
1914. I am not one of these children and I really do not
remember being in a class or school picture while I was
there.

My name was Marion Morrison and I had to ride to school
on horseback. The horse developed a disease that kept it
skinny. We finally had to destroy it but the nosey biddies
of the town called the humane society and accused me, a
7 year-old, of not feeding my horse and watering him. This
was proven in time to be a lie. I think it was occasioned by
the fact that I had allowed a boy even younger than myself to
get on the horse and ride him the full length of the town-from
one telephone pole to the next-and he fell off the horse which did
not upset him but it upset the dear ladies of Lancaster. Anyway,
that incident may be found in the annals of your town news and/or
remembered gossip. As a matter of fact because the horse was
so skinny, I was called skinny which I wish I were today. If there
are any other pictures that might be 1914, I would certainly enjoy
receiving one, but I have a pretty good memory and I do not remember having my picture taken while at Lancaster Grammar School.

Please accept the statements in this letter as humor and as not
being disparaging. Often times a person writes something intended
for fun and it is mis-interpreted. This was written for my enjoy-
ment and I hope yours.

Sincerely,

John Wayne

P.S. The statements are correct.

(Courtesy of the Academy of Motion Picture Arts and Sciences)

"HE'S A WARM, KIND-HEARTED, LOVING, GENEROUS, INTELLECTUAL GENIUS."

— *Actress Deborah Kerr*

A PRIVATE LIFE PUBLIC

Chata Bauer frantically paced back and forth across the floor of the massive living room in the home she shared with John Wayne. It was late. She backhanded a wave of silky, black hair out of her eyes and pulled her designer robe tightly around her shapely figure. Her cheeks were stained with tears, and the makeup she used to cover the blemishes on her face was streaked. When Chata called the party to find out where Wayne was, she was told that he was escorting Gail home—a considerable distance from the Wayne residence. Chata was outraged, and the later the hour grew, the more it fueled her suspicions. By the time Wayne arrived at the house, she was convinced he was involved with Gail Russell and she was ready to kill him over it.

Chata checked the clock over the fireplace for the millionth time and headed to the bar in the corner of the room. After pouring herself a glass of bourbon and stirring it with her finger, she downed the drink in one swallow. A picture of she and Duke together with their dogs caught her eye. She picked up the photo, cursed her husband in Spanish, then threw the framed print against the wall. The glass shattered.

John Wayne had married Chata Bauer on January 18, 1946. Chata had hoped her new husband would devote a substantial amount of his time solely to her, but Wayne had to work. He was a highly sought-after actor who thrived on making movies. By mid-1946 Duke was looking forward to starring in a full roster of motion pictures. Less than a year into their marriage, his commitment to his work and the time he spent with the leading ladies in his films had Chata feeling neglected, lonely, and resentful. The empty bottles of alcohol that littered the room were evidence of her frustration over the lack of attention.

Several pages of a phone book lay strewn over the coffee table. She had called everyone she could think of looking for her husband. Just as she made her way to the phone, picked up the receiver and started to dial another number, the doorbell rang. Wayne was on the other side trying to get into the house, but the door was locked. He jiggled the handle, rang the bell

Duke poses with his second wife, Chata Bauer, and their dogs at their home in Encino, California, in 1946. *(Courtesy of the Academy of Motion Picture Arts and Sciences)*

again, and pounded on the wooden frame. He yelled for Chata to let him in, but she refused. She cursed at him, returned to the bar, poured herself another drink, and proceeded down the hallway toward her bedroom.

After a few moments, Wayne's persistent shouts for someone to let him in stopped. All was quiet for a moment and then a few of the glass panes around the door shattered. Wayne's sturdy fist reached in through the broken window and unlocked the door. He then dragged his weary frame to the couch and plopped down.

He could hear Chata and her mother, Esperanza, speaking in hushed, angry tones in the other room. He knew there would be hell to pay for his late arrival home. He was resting his eyes, waiting for the inevitable confrontation when Chata burst into the room carrying a loaded automatic weapon that she pointed at Wayne, threatening to kill him. Esperanza followed and pulled on Chata's arm, trying to talk some sense into her. Chata jerked away from her mother and trained the barrel of the gun on her husband.

Wayne jumped to his feet as Chata hurled accusations at him. She was certain that he was having an affair with actress Gail Russell, his costar in the movie he was shooting, *Angel and the Badman*. Wayne denied the allegations while Esperanza shouted for Chata to put away the gun. Eventually she laid the .45 on the bar and the three dispersed to their separate rooms to sleep off the memory of the battle.

This peaceful domestic scene with Duke, his wife, and her mother, belied their tumultous relationship. *(Courtesy of the Academy of Motion Picture Arts and Sciences)*

Duke had met the fiery, Latin beauty who would be his second wife in Mexico in 1941. He had made the trip with his business manager, Bo Roos, and a few of Roos's clients, including actors Ward Bond, Fred MacMurray, and Ray Milland. The purpose of the journey was to look over investment opportunities, one of which was a motion-picture studio. Churubusco Studios was the leading production company in Mexico. Not only was the facility with its movie equipment and film library for sale, but a stable of talent accompanied the business. Chata

Bauer was a twenty-year-old actress contracted with the studio who had been romantically involved with Ray Milland for some time.

Chata boldly introduced herself to Wayne at a luncheon hosted by the president of Churubusco Studios for the potential buyers. Wayne was captivated by her infectious personality, scintillating good looks, and her interest in his career. Milland was one of the first to recognize that Wayne and Chata were attracted to one another. He was not initially threatened by their mutual admiration. Wayne was married, after all, and he believed the smitten pair would not act on their feelings.

Wayne and Chata's paths would cross again at a dinner party thrown by Roos a few days later. They seized the chance to get to know one another better and found they had a lot in common. They shared a similar outlook on the basic essentials of life. Chata presented herself as a woman who craved a simple living surrounded by children and friends. After the two finished their meal, they danced a little and then went for a walk on the beach. Their evening ended with a promise to meet the following day and go horseback riding.

The riding date proved to be a delightful experience for both. Chata was a fine horsewoman and possessed many other qualities Wayne appreciated. Like him she enjoyed swimming, hunting, and fishing. Those interests, combined with Wayne's natural inclination for Latin women, convinced him that Chata might be his perfect match.

The more time the two spent together, the more Wayne's infatuation with Chata grew. She seemed to say all the right things to win his affection. For the remainder of the time Wayne was in Mexico, he and Chata never left each other's side. By the time he departed, the two had fallen in love.

Once he returned home, the 34-year-old Wayne could think of nothing but Chata and began making plans to bring her to Hollywood. After viewing a few of the motion pictures Chata had appeared in, Wayne decided that he would approach Republic executives about hiring the actress on for the studio.

Rumor of Wayne's affair had followed him back to the States, and his wife Josephine learned about his infidelity. The news hurt her deeply. She asked Wayne about the rumor, and he didn't deny his feelings for Chata. He wanted a divorce, but Josephine refused to give him one. Frustrated, he moved out of their home and into his own place.

Two years and several trips to Mexico later, Wayne finally managed to have the tempestuous Chata relocated to California. Josephine was humiliated. Gossip columnists and the tabloids relentlessly reported on Wayne and Chata's relationship, eventually prompting Josephine to file for a legal separation.

As a way to combat the negative press surrounding his top star, Herbert Yates granted Chata a screen test, put Chata on the payroll, and helped her acquire a visa to remain in the United States. The focus on the front page of many trade papers shifted from Wayne's romantic life to Chata as a budding new talent. However, most of Chata's time at Republic was not spent making movies but instead following Wayne to the set of his films and staying with him. The two were inseparable on and off the lot. They boldly flaunted their romance in public and even shared a posh apartment on Sunset Boulevard. In late 1944 Josephine gave in and filed for divorce.

Duke and Josephine's divorce was officially over on Christmas Day, 1945. Three weeks after Wayne's marriage to Josephine was legally dissolved, he and Chata were headed to the altar. The ceremony took place at the Unity Presbyterian Church in Long Beach, California. Herbert Yates gave the bride away and Ward Bond was the best man.

The newlyweds gave an interview to *Photoplay Magazine* in February 1946 and expressed the deep devotion they had for one another. Chata announced that she would be giving up her acting pursuits so that she could be available for her husband whenever he needed her. Wayne was moved by the sacrifice and pleased that her focus would be entirely on him.

It wasn't until well after Wayne and Chata took their vows that he realized how influential his wife's mother would be in their lives. Mother and daughter were very close and could not bear to be far apart from one another. Chata wept often because she missed her mother. Once Wayne and Chata returned from their honeymoon in Hawaii, Wayne invited Esperanza to live with them. She happily accepted her offer.

Wayne's mother-in-law's constant presence became a source of tension between the newlyweds.

For several years John Wayne's personal life was in flux, but his professional life was anything but. He continued to improve as an actor, and the film projects he was offered left a lasting impression on movie-going audiences. Less than a month after he and Chata were married, he began production on his fourth John Ford film, a war picture entitled *They Were Expendable*. Immediately following the picture he starred in *Without Reservations* opposite Claudette Colbert.

Wayne's busy schedule left little quality time with his new bride, and Chata was becoming increasingly unhappy as a result. Wayne worked twelve- and fourteen-hour days and his coworkers were some of Hollywood's loveliest actresses. Chata was resentful of those ladies because they were seeing more of her husband than she was. Her insecurities gave way to the suspicion that the relationship Wayne had with his female co-stars was not strictly business. She attempted to drown her uncertainties with alcohol, but that only had the effect of making them seem more plausible. The fact that Chata was unable to conceive a child added to her misery.

Esperanza helped fuel the hurt and mistrust by insinuating that Wayne might be having an affair. She convinced her daughter that no actor and actress could pretend to be in love on the screen if there weren't some real emotion between them

Angel and the Badman was Wayne's first film as producer. *(Courtesy of the Academy of Motion Picture Arts and Sciences)*

to motivate their actions. Chata's suspicions were particularly focused on actress Gail Russell and the romantic scenes she and Wayne worked on in the Western *Angel and the Badman*.

Russell was a twenty-one-year-old, angel-faced beauty who played the part of a Quaker girl who nursed Wayne back to health after he was shot. Wayne befriended Russell on the set and took a particular, big-brother kind of interest in her life. She had a problem with alcohol, and Wayne, who was not only the lead in the movie but the film's producer as well, wanted to help see her through the shooting of the picture sober.

Chata misinterpreted Wayne's kind gesture. No matter how many times he and Gail Russell insisted their feelings did not extend beyond that of a brother-sister type of relationship, Chata would not accept the truth.

On the night that Wayne busted the window to get into his house and Chata greeted him with a loaded handgun, Wayne had hosted a party to celebrate finalizing production on *Angel and the Badman* and to reward the cast and crew for their hard work. At the end of the evening, he had driven Gail to her apartment and then headed on to his own home.

The volatile incident passed, but it scarred their marriage. Both began drinking more and more as a way to cope with their stormy, passionate relationship. In an attempt to make a fresh start, Wayne moved his wife and mother-in-law out of the small ranch house they were renting in Van Nuys into a magnificent twelve-room, two-story home in Encino. For a short time they were happy. Chata busied herself decorating their place, and Wayne continued working.

After a few months Esperanza starting causing trouble again. She frequently encouraged Chata to have a more than few cocktails with her. The two would spend days drinking. Wayne, or one of the members of the house staff, would have to care for them until they were sober again. Wayne was disgusted with his wife's behavior. Chata was a mean drunk, and Wayne's own temper would only tolerate so many insults and violent outbursts before he would explode.

In December 1946 Wayne persuaded Chata to leave her mother behind and to travel to Hawaii with him for a much-needed rest. They both hoped the time away at the place where they spent their honeymoon would do their marriage good. However, excessive drinking on both of their parts led to another major argument. The verbal altercation turned physical. When the incident was brought up in court during their divorce proceedings, Chata claimed Wayne was the aggressor. Wayne admitted to getting "rough with her" but said she antagonized him.

Chata worked hard at getting the kind of forceful attention she received from Wayne. She had numerous affairs and often flaunted her lovers in her husband's face. The result was an increase in violent episodes between the two and a desire to drown their unhappiness in alcohol.

The war of the Waynes lasted five years through several of Duke's attempts to try and save the union. His final effort to salvage their relationship occurred in mid-1952. He returned home after work one evening, anxious to talk things out with Chata, and instead came face to face with a private investigator. Esperanza had hired the man to keep Wayne away from her daughter. Chata and Duke's fights had often become physical, and Duke had defended himself from Chata's kicks and pummeling fists by holding her arms and legs firmly down until she was calm. The bruises on Chata's wrists and ankles where Duke had grabbed her led Esperanza to believe he would seriously hurt her daughter. The private investigator she hired had orders to shoot Duke should he come on the property.

Unaware that his life was in danger, Wayne returned home. He managed to make his way into the house because the private investigator had fallen asleep on the job. The butler informed Duke that Chata was out for the evening, and he decided to wait in the den until she came home. After a few hours Wayne dozed off to sleep. He was awakened by the sound of a gun being cocked. When he opened his eyes he was staring down the barrel of a rifle. The private investigator was persuaded not to shoot, and Wayne left the house without seeing Chata.

Chata filed for a divorce from Wayne in the spring of 1953. The private life and heartbreak of the popular actor was publicized in papers across the country. Chata claimed Wayne emotionally and physically abused her and demanded $9,000 a month in temporary alimony. The amount included a stipend for her mother. Wayne's attorney, Frank Belcher, called the charges and Chata's financial requests "outrageous." The unusual matter was argued before a Superior Court judge and printed in the papers long before the divorce was finalized:

> What legal obligation has a husband to continue supporting his mother-in-law after separation from his wife?
>
> This was a question brought up yesterday in the current alimony hearing of film actor John Wayne and his Mexican born wife Chata, in the Superior Court of Judge William R. McKay.

Mrs. Wayne testified that during the six years of her married life with the actor she spent $650 a month for the support of her mother in Mexico. This amount, she implied through her attorney, should be taken into account when temporary alimony is fixed by the court pending trial of the Wayne divorce.

She is asking $9000 a month. Attorney Frank Belcher, for Wayne, has made a tentative counter offer of $900 a month. Mrs. Wayne told the court that prior to and during her marriage her husband repeatedly assured her that funds would continue to go to her mother.

Judge McKay expressed doubt as to the validity of the claim, thus siding with objections of Attorney Belcher. "If Mr. Wayne contracted such an obligation then the mother-in-law, not the wife, must enforce it," said Belcher.

In a tentative ruling the jurist said he knew of no legal precedent establishing the necessity of a man supporting his mother-in-law.

Hollywood Citizen-News—March 26, 1953

Wayne and his estranged wife bared their souls and finances when the divorce hearing began on May 19, 1953. He was forced to provide the court with a detailed account of his income and expenditures. Chata claimed Wayne had millions, but his income tax statements showed the two spent most of what he made. Duke was embarrassed by the admission and told the judge hearing the case that Chata was responsible for the depletion of their funds. "My manager told her he wanted us to live on a budget," Wayne offered. "But she refused."

Chata's attorney, Jerome Rosenthal countered with a list of expenditures the two shared that included a monthly allowance for gifts, clothing, jewelry, and personal effects totaling $5,160.

After Chata testified about their financial situation she launched into accusations that Duke was a "wife beater." Wayne strongly denied the claim. The newspapers printed everything the pair said about one another.

> John Wayne, the 6-foot, 4-inch "he-man," yesterday told a judge in alimony court that his wife, who wants $9,350 monthly temporary alimony, frequently "manhandled" him.
>
> The subject of marriage violence came up when counsel for the former Mexican actress Chata Bauer Wayne asked Superior Judge William R. McKay to restrain Wayne from "molesting" her.
>
> "Did you ever strike your wife?" Attorney Jerome Rosenthal asked the 225-pound former University of Southern California football player.
>
> "I never at any time during our marriage struck my wife," retorted Wayne. "I will add that many times I had to protect myself from her temper—I call it manhandling. Many times I had to hold her arms and grab her foot when she was trying to strike or kick me.
>
> *Los Angeles Daily News*—June 2, 1953

Wayne endured two weeks of grueling cross-examination about his private life. Several times he wanted to drop out of the entire proceeding, pay Chata what she wanted, and get on with his life. His attorney convinced him to continue fighting.

New and compelling information about Chata was soon to be revealed.

During the end of the second week of the trial, one of the members of Wayne's household staff came forward with information about a guest Chata had while Duke was away on business. Nicky Hilton, son of hotel magnate Conrad Hilton, ex-husband of actress Elizabeth Taylor and man about town, had spent several nights with Chata at Wayne's home. The servant had saved a few scribblings Mrs. Wayne made and had thrown in the trash. She had scribbled Nick and Chata, Chata Hilton and Mrs. Nick Hilton on a piece of paper. When asked about the matter in court, Chata assured the judge that she meant nothing by what she wrote and that she and Nick were merely friends.

After a fifteen-day trial, the Waynes were granted a divorce based on the grounds of mutual recrimination. Duke agreed to pay Chata an initial lump settlement of $150,000 and an additional $50,000 a year for six years.

When it was all over, Chata and her mother returned to Mexico. John Wayne went on with his movie making. Two of his most successful films were released during the time the divorce was in process. In spite of his personal hardships, *Hondo* and *The Quiet Man* earned the actor the coveted title of top box-office attraction.

"It was a miserable chapter in my life," Wayne told biographer Maurice Zolotow in 1971. "It's often been said that an actor lives in the limelight and so he mustn't be surprised when his troubles are made more of than other people's."

Wayne had limited contact with Chata once she relocated. Thirteen months after the divorce was finalized she was found dead in her hotel room in Mexico City from a massive heart attack brought on by acute alcoholism.

Chata's tragic death and indeed the relationship as a whole left Wayne exhausted and feeling guilty for how her life ended. Fellow actor and friend Paul Fix encouraged Wayne to "press on and concentrate on the things he had some control over, namely his film career." It was advice Wayne enthusiastically took.

———

"HE'S NOT SOMETHING OUT OF A
BOOK, GOVERNED BY ACTING RULES.
HE PORTRAYS JOHN WAYNE, A RUGGED
AMERICAN GUY. HE'S NOT ONE OF THOSE
METHOD ACTORS, LIKE THEY SEND OUT
HERE FROM DRAMA SCHOOLS IN NEW
YORK. HE'S REAL, PERFECTLY NATURAL."

— *Director John Ford*

THE COWBOY
IS AN ACTOR

A hot noonday sun hung high in the sky. A dusty breeze pushed through a stand of 9,000 head of cattle grazing in the deep grass under the flinty apron of rock jutting out of the hills. Several sweat-soaked cowboys circled the herd on horseback, making sure the animals were safe from predators and rustlers. Their duties were momentarily interrupted when four rogue cowboys rode up on the stand. The gruff-looking men rode passed the wranglers and made their way to a nearby camp.

Cattleman Tom Dunson watched the four cowhands dismount and walk their rides toward him. The spectacular, sprawling landscape stretched out behind them. Dunson eyed the men carefully. He was angry and his rifle was close at hand. The cowboys cautiously dismounted. They'd committed the cardinal sin of leaving the cattle drive early. Lives and livestock had been jeopardized. They expected a tongue lashing but feared Dunson would do more. "I don't like quitters," Dunson tells them. "Especially when they're not good enough to finish what they started."

––––––––

Screenwriter Borden Chase wrote the line, but it was John Wayne who delivered it with the heated intensity needed to make it sound ominous. Wayne's portrayal of the ruthless, contemptible rancher in the movie *Red River* inspired generations of actors, from Marlon Brando to Brad Pitt. Critics not only praised his performance as exceptional but considered the film itself to be the best Western ever made. Film historians cite the gruff dialogue, distinguished acting, inspired setting, and outstanding direction as reasons that the movie remains a classic.

John Wayne did not begin his film career with an innate talent for acting. In an interview with *Motion Picture Magazine* in 1931, Wayne admitted to a lack of skill at the start of his career. "I knew there was no use trying to act," he said, "because I didn't know a thing about it. But I figured that if they liked me as I am—just being natural—I'd get along all right."

Audiences did like his natural approach to the craft, and the favorable response inspired Wayne to allow his raw abilities to be shaped by the motion-picture greats he came in contact with.

Not long after being cast in his first major film, *The Big Trail*, Duke began taking acting lessons from a Shakespearean drama coach. He learned the basics: proper voice inflection, how to memorize and deliver lines, when to smile, and how to carry himself. The results weren't completely positive. On the first day of rehearsals for *The Big Trail*, Wayne's mannerisms and style were greatly exaggerated. Director Rauol Walsh intervened. He instructed Wayne to talk slower, make smaller moves, and always look the person he was acting opposite in the eye. "He spent two weeks working the ham out of me," Wayne shared with fans in 1952.

Producers and directors who worked with Wayne appreciated the effort he put into his job. They complimented him on knowing his lines and being on time. Few had the heart to chastise Wayne for making any mistakes on camera, because he was always the first to be aware of them. If he felt he had done poorly in a particular scene or had not delivered the dialogue properly, he would give himself a stern talking to. He strived to be better with every take and with every new project.

Paul Fix, who at the time of his death in 1983 had more than 300 films to his credit, helped Wayne develop his acting technique. John Ford introduced the two, and Fix took Wayne under his wing and taught him basic movement skills, what to do with his hands while talking, and how to really listen to the other actors in each scene.

Fix devised a series of hand signals to give Wayne when the cameras started to roll. The signals reminded Duke not to overdo furrowing his brow, raising his eyebrows, or shifting his weight unnecessarily from hip to hip. Fix worked with Wayne for years, but few ever noticed the secret code between the student and teacher.

Wayne credited Fix with helping him create his unforgettable swagger. When Duke confided in Fix that he didn't care for the way he looked as he walked on screen, the two decided to change his gait. Fix suggested that Wayne point his toes into the ground as he walked. The movement forced his shoulders and hips to sway in a distinctive fashion that added an extra something to the saunter. It was something no one else did or could effectively duplicate.

Wayne's acting was influenced by many of the thespians he appeared with in films. From Harry Carey, he learned the cadence he used when speaking—how to pause for effect at just the right time in mid-sentence. Yakima Canutt taught him how to show true emotion. Montgomery Clift exemplified the dramatic intensity he employed in movies like *The Searchers* and *Hondo*.

Clift was twenty-eight years old when he costarred in *Red River* with Wayne. He was a veteran of Broadway, but *Red River* was his first feature film. The film spanned a fifteen-year period and Wayne played the part of Clift's (Matthew Garth) adopted

Duke portrayed a cattle baron in the 1948 film *Red River*, co-starring Montgomery Clift. *(Courtesy of the Academy of Motion Picture Arts and Sciences)*

Red River, directed by Howard Hawks, was one of Duke's favorite films. *(Courtesy of the Academy of Motion Picture Arts and Sciences)*

father. Gary Cooper was originally cast as the lead in the picture, but he had turned down the part John Wayne eventually accepted. Cooper felt the character was not likable enough. Wayne felt differently about the role. He attacked the part, displaying a range of emotions that prompted director John Ford to remark after seeing the film, "I didn't know the son-of-a-bitch could act."

Howard Hawks directed *Red River*. With a budget of $3 million, it was the most expensive film Wayne had ever been a part of. It became one of the highest grossing films of 1948. It was one of Duke's favorite films. As a symbol of his fondness for the movie, he never made another picture with Hawks without wearing the "Red River D" belt he wore in *Red River*.

Among Wayne's peers who appreciated his talent was Katharine Hepburn. In an interview with *Daily Variety* in 1969, Hepburn described the actor as a "man with an extraordinary gift. He has a very subtle capacity to think and caress the camera—the audience—with no apparent effort."

Many of Wayne's co-workers agreed with Hepburn's assessment of his skill. Howard Hawks told people that Wayne was a "superb actor because you can't catch him at it."

In an interview with *Hollywood Citizens News* in 1951, Wayne shared his approach to acting with reporter Lowell Redelings. "I read dramatic lines under dramatically," he told him, "and react to situations normally. It isn't as simple as it sounds. I've spent a major portion of my life trying to learn to do it well and I'm not past learning yet."

The films released in 1948 and 1949 were further examples of how fine an actor Wayne had become. In movies like *3 Godfathers*, *Fort Apache*, and *She Wore A Yellow Ribbon*, he mastered the craft Katharine Hepburn referred to as "total reality performing"

"He got to a point then," Hepburn told *Daily Variety*, "where the acting does not appear to be acting, and becomes as powerful as his personality."

3 Godfathers, *Fort Apache*, and *She Wore A Yellow Ribbon* were all directed by John Ford. After seeing Wayne's performance in *Red River*, Ford had gained a new-found respect for his protégé's acting. According to Ford, Wayne was now a "great actor because he was the same off the screen as he was playing the part."

Ford's high praise signaled a change in their working relationship. He no longer felt the need to be as forceful with the actor in order to get the performance from him he wanted. Ford found other victims to intimidate, and Duke took it upon himself to come to the aid of those actors.

During the filming of *Fort Apache*, Ford targeted John Agar, who portrayed 2nd Lieutenant Michael Shannon O'Rourke. Ford treated Agar in much the same way he had treated Wayne when he first went to work for him. After enduring several days of Ford's harsh treatment, Agar contemplated leaving the movie. Wayne talked his young costar into staying and shared his personal experiences with Ford. He explained the motivation behind Ford's insults and assured him that the director's

In the late 1940s, Duke created some of his most memorable roles. Here he is in *Fort Apache* with John Agar, Shirley Temple, and Henry Fonda. *(Courtesy of the Academy of Motion Picture Arts and Sciences)*

intention was simply to help Agar deliver the "best perform-ance and become a fine actor."

Agar reluctantly agreed to stick it out. Wayne worked with him by running lines and gave him horseback-riding tips. Duke helped him deliver the performance Ford was seeking, and Agar was forever indebted to Wayne.

Harry Carey Jr. went through the same kind of torment with Ford during the filming of 3 Godfathers. Again, Wayne saw the frustrated actor through the ordeal. Ford had been good friends with Carey's father, Harry Carey Sr., and was brokenhearted over the cowboy actor's death just months prior to shooting 3 Godfathers. Harry Carey Jr. had worked with Ford in the past, but this was Carey's first chance to star in one of Ford's pic-tures. Ford was overly tough on Carey and consistently brought up actor Audie Murphy's name as a replacement for him. Carey decided to quit the film, but Duke stopped him.

"He convinced me that Mr. Ford was trying to get me riled up to get a performance out of me," Carey told Wayne biogra-pher Maurice Zolotow. "Duke told me that as far as he was con-cerned, I was a good man and worthy to carry my father's name. He saved my life."

Not only did Wayne assist other actors and actresses in the films with him with creative tips but he provided them with an example of a strong work ethic. He arrived to the set on time, listened attentively to the director, and always knew his lines.

Wayne took great pride in being a part of the motion-picture industry and his work reflected that. In an interview for *The Hollywood Scene* in October 1951, Wayne said his association with movies was a "source of enormous joy. . . . It gives me a genuine feeling of satisfaction to have a part in the tremendous job this industry does in creating entertainment on a scale no other medium can even attempt," he boasted. "I like my job, I like the people I work with, and I have the highest respect for what the screen accomplishes, and what it stands for."

John Wayne's pride in his job was clearly exhibited in 1949. The three films he starred in that year made more than $15 million combined. On September 15, 1949, the first of two Wayne Westerns were released. *The Fighting Kentuckian*, costarring Oliver Hardy and Vera Ralston, was the story of a bluff trapper who romances a beautiful French woman while foiling a land-grab scheme in the process. The movie received very few good reviews, but it made a great deal of money.

The following month R.K.O. released the classic picture *She Wore A Yellow Ribbon*. Wayne played retiring Cavalry Captain Nathan Brittles. Critics commended Duke's performance in the role, which was unlike any other in his career to that point. The moments his character spent talking to his deceased wife at her gravesite were touching without being overly sentimental. The film was honored by the Writer's Guild of America and named Best Written American Western, and the Academy

Wayne sits tall in the saddle in the John Ford classic, *She Wore a Yellow Ribbon*, released in 1948. *(Courtesy of the Academy of Motion Picture Arts and Sciences)*

of Motion Picture Arts and Sciences gave director of photography Winton Hoch the award for best cinematography.

Duke believed his work in *She Wore A Yellow Ribbon* was his finest acting achievement. According to the biography *Shooting Star,* Wayne hoped his contemporaries would recognize the effort with an Oscar nomination, but that didn't happen. He speculated the reason to be was that his peers did not consider the kind of acting he did to be acting at all. "Nobody seems to like my acting but the people," Duke lamented.

Wayne followed up his exceptional performance in *She Wore A Yellow Ribbon* with the brilliant portrayal of Sergeant John M. Stryker in *Sands of Iwo Jima.* The gripping war drama, directed by Allan Dwan, was a commercial success. Hollywood also took notice of the job Wayne did in the picture with an Academy Award nomination for Best Actor. Wayne was proud and appreciative. "The *Sands of Iwo Jima* was a beautiful, personal story," he told reporters at the Oscar ceremony on March 23, 1950. "It's the story of a sergeant who whips young recruits into shape. It's Mr. Chips put in the military." Other actors nominated in the same category as Wayne were Broderick Crawford, Kirk Douglas, Gregory Peck, and Richard Todd. Broderick Crawford took home the prize for his role in *All the King's Men.*

Over the next twenty-nine years, Wayne's acting continued to get better. He delivered remarkable and memorable performances

This advertisement for *She Wore a Yellow Ribbon* appeared in *Picturegoers Magazine*. (Courtesy of the Academy of Motion Picture Arts and Sciences)

in *The Searchers*, *The Quiet Man*, *The Man Who Shot Liberty Valance*, and *The Longest Day*. His second Academy Award nomination came in 1969 for his role as the overweight, over-the-hill U.S. Marshal in *True Grit*. The *New York Times* proclaimed that Wayne delivered "the richest performance of his long career." *The Atlantic Monthly* praised Wayne's part noting that "he is a hell of a good actor who obviously took great relish in the opportunity to play a meaty role." After forty years in the motion picture business, Wayne was awarded the Oscar. *The Los Angeles Herald Examiner* called it a "fitting tribute."

After the Academy Award ceremony, motion-picture industry leaders confessed that they had underrated Wayne as an actor for too long. Director Howard Hawks agreed and defensively added, "All the sudden they're saying he's a good actor. Well, he always was."

LOOKING AT HOLLYWOOD
WITH HEDDA HOPPER

The following article was written by celebrity gossip columnist, Hedda Hopper in February 1949. It was one of eight articles she wrote about John Wayne. All are on file at the Academy of Motion Picture Arts and Sciences in Los Angeles.

Press agents, mothers, presidents of fan clubs, agents, best friends and critics invariably want to come along with the stars on my Sunday interviews, but I always try to turn on the tact so that I can talk to 'em alone.

You may be able to understand the problem when I tell you of my exchange with John (Duke) Wayne, who was accompanied by a publicity man from the studio.

———————

"Well," I began, "You're suddenly becoming Hollywood's hardest working actor, aren't you?"

"I guess I'm pitching for the record." Wayne said. "I've finished three pictures in less than the last six months, *3 Godfathers, She Wore A Yellow Ribbon,* and now, *Witch."*

The correct title of that picture is Republic productions *The Wake of the Red Witch,* the press agent interposed with a Cheshire grin.

Wayne and I both fixed him for a long moment with acid stares, but the smile seemed to be glued on.

"None of this one-picture-a-year stuff for you?" I suggested.

Duke laughed. "Listen, I've got to work for my living. I don't have a capital gains setup like some of these guys, and I've got two families to feed. My business manager tells it me it costs me $2,600 a month. I don't know where the money goes, but it's an awful lot, and I've got to keep hopping from Republic to RKO to Argosy to make it."

"You've been starring in pictures for twenty-two straight years and you've made more than eighty. If you had a record like that in show business or selling groceries or as a doctor you'd be entitled to retire now with a nice nest egg," I said.

"That's true," he answered, "But I look at it this way. Actors aren't supposed to be business men, and I guess I'm luckier than most that I do have something to show for it. I've got a few oil wells, and I own the Flatiron building in Culver City and part of a country club, and I've got a finger in a couple of other things.

—————

"The word 'retire' sounds great, but I'd only be honest with myself by admitting that I get a terrific bang out of my work, playing an interesting script and all the associations."

"Yeah, Duke, tell her what a great company there was on *The Wake of the Red Witch*," the press agent was in again.

"Of course," Wayne went on, "my most wonderful friend is John Ford. It's an old story, but I was a prop man for him earning some of the folding stuff while I was playing football for the University of Southern California. They'd always ask how you crouched to buck the line, and then they'd trip you. It was a corny joke, but I always tried to be patient. Ford tried it, and I went flat on my face in the mud. I said, 'Let's try it again,' only this time I turned suddenly and let him have my foot right where it would do the most good.

This was daring with an important director, but Ford loved it. Then on location at Catalina, five big actors were supposed to take a dive from a ship into the Pacific for an important shot. Ford turned to me and said, 'Jump, Wayne.' All five refused to do it. I dived five times for five different guys in long shots, and Ford made me an actor from that day on.

Whenever I've been in trouble, he's always been there. During the war he was in Washington with the navy and I got into a mess. He flew out here, got me, took me back, and made me spend a week with him. He didn't ask me anything, he didn't tell my anything. That's what I call a friend."

"It's nice to talk to an actor who remembers to be grateful," I said. "Let me see. What shall I ask you now?"

"Why don't you ask him how he liked working in *The Wake of the Red Witch*," the press agent interposed. I made up my mind I might have to do something about this lad.

"Duke, did you ever give any thought to going on stage?"

"No, that's completely out for me. It's a different racket altogether, I think. I think it may be good for newcomers, but only because it gives them a certain confidence and poise. But, to me, screen acting is reacting. You come on the screen in a given situation, and the audience wants to see how you handle yourself. I think I work best in front of a camera."

After seeing several of Wayne's movies myself, I think he does well in front of a camera too. And I'm sure that goes double for the job he did in *The Wake of the Red Witch*.

(Article reprinted with the permission of the Chicago Tribune*)*

"THERE IS NO ONE WHO MORE EXEMPLIFIES
THE DEVOTION TO OUR COUNTRY, ITS
GOODNESS, ITS INDUSTRY, AND ITS
STRENGTHS THAN JOHN WAYNE."

— *President Ronald Reagan*

CIVIC-MINDED DUKE

Flamboyant, outspoken gossip columnist Hedda Hopper approached the podium at the Hollywood American Legion and stared out over a sea of faces. The majority of the people watching her were influential leaders in the movie business who had assembled for a regular meeting of the Motion Picture Alliance for the Preservation of American Ideals in April 1951.

The organization's president, John Wayne, introduced Hopper to the crowd. She had asked for a chance to address the group on a matter of profound importance. Wayne graciously accommodated her. It wasn't unusual for members to request a moment to speak on a topic they wanted the alliance to consider. Wayne was unaware that the issue Hopper wanted to discuss was the actor himself. As a round of polite applause rose up, Duke headed back to his seat on the dais. Hopper stopped him before he could get too far away and pulled him back towards the lectern. Wayne smiled obligingly.

————————

Wayne had been a member of the Motion Picture Alliance almost from the beginning of its inception in the late 1940s when directors Sam Wood, Walt Disney, and Leo McCarey had founded the group to protect the movie profession from the perceived threat of Communism to the American way of life. The Communist Party was a growing political force in the United States in the 1930s and 1940s. But after World War II, a wide-ranging anti-Communist network had developed to lead the nation on a crusade against domestic Communism.

In October 1947 a number of suspected Communists working in the Hollywood film industry were summoned to appear before the House Un-American Activities Committee (HUAC), which was investigating Communist influence in Hollywood labor unions. The Motion Picture Alliance was a major force of the anti-Communism network that sought to stop the impact of the party. Part of the group's statement of principles included a commitment "to fight with every means at our organized command, any effort of any group or individual to divert the loyalty of the screen from the free America that gave it birth."

Many Hollywood actors, writers, and producers were called before the HUAC. Gary Cooper, Robert Montgomery, George Murphy, and Ronald Reagan testified, named names, and encouraged Congress to intervene in what they saw as the growing presence of Communists in the motion picture industry. Suspected or known communists were frequently "blacklisted" by studios, or put on lists of writers, actors, and other industry professionals who were no longer to be hired.

The majority of the members of the Motion Picture Alliance for the Preservation of American Ideals, who included many high-profile conservatives, such as Clark Gable, Gary Cooper, and Ward Bond, were in favor of "blacklisting" or barring members of the Communist Party from jobs in the motion-picture industry both on-screen and behind the scenes.

Although Wayne believed in maintaining the American ideals in film, he was not in favor of blacklisting. He felt that denying a person the right to work based on their political orientation was wrong. He was also tolerant of industry professionals once associated with the Communist Party who apologized and asked for a second chance.

Wayne was never asked to appear before the committee, but his idol Harry Carey was not as fortunate. Carey refused to be manipulated by the committee chair, Joseph McCarthy, who wanted those who testified to make untrue statements about fellow actors he hoped to imprison. Carey would not go along with him. His uncooperative attitude led to his own blacklisting.

Wayne's understanding attitude did not sit well with many of the members of the alliance. The majority believed the best way to fight the Communist influence was to bar party members from jobs in front of and behind the screen. The situation that angered Hedda Hopper and brought Wayne a fair amount of criticism concerned actor Larry Parks.

In 1951, Parks had been called before the House Un-American Activities Committee and extensively questioned about his involvement with the Communist Party. He admitted to being a member of the party and expressed his deep regret over the association. He then cooperated with the committee in its quest to find out who else was involved with the movement. Parks gave the committee several names of other participants. Although he was never officially blacklisted, Columbia Pictures terminated his contract, and other studios refused to work with him as well.

Leaders of the HUAC asked Wayne, as president of the Motion Picture Alliance, to comment on Parks's actions. Duke's response was not the harsh reply they expected. He called Parks's behavior courageous and added that he needed moral support. "He should be commended as a good American."

Few in the Alliance agreed with Wayne.

At the Motion Picture Alliance April meeting in 1951, Hopper gave Duke a thorough tongue lashing at one of the regular meetings of the alliance. She called him a "damn fool" for supporting Parks. Wayne hotly defended his position and added, "when any member of the party breaks with them, we must welcome him back into American society. We should give him friendship and help him find employment again in our industry."

The reaction from the Alliance members at the end of the Hopper–Wayne exchange was mixed. Some were irritated with Hopper's open criticism of Wayne while others commended her firm position. After much discussion the conservative and liberal sides of the Alliance decided that all its members would withhold any comments on the HUAC hearings until the complete facts were known.

According to director John Farrow, who worked with Wayne on the movie *Hondo*, Duke's politics revolved around a simple issue: "he felt protective of his country and its way of life." In spite of the fact that Duke had a soft heart for those who had made personal mistakes, he was less forgiving of filmmakers who produced material that denounced America's heritage and foundation, which was perhaps what motivated him to participate in the Alliance. Among the directors and producers he strongly objected to were Academy Award winners Robert Rossen and Stanley Kramer.

Wayne felt that Rossen's film *All the King's Men* and Kramer's movie *High Noon* were patently "un-American." *All the King's Men* is the story of the rise of politician Willie Stark. Duke believed that the majority of the characters in Rossen's motion picture lacked moral fiber. The character of Stark was a shady leader who seems only to benefit from his corrupt ways. Duke believed that character fully demonstrated to young viewers that doing right is pointless and evil has great rewards.

Duke also felt that Kramer's *High Noon* possessed the "single most disrespectful act in any film to date." At the end of the movie, Gary Cooper's character removes his United States Marshal's badge, tosses it into the street and steps on it as he walks away. "The message was clear and disturbing to me. It was like belittling the Medal of Honor," Wayne told biographer Maurice Zolotow.

In an effort to counteract the negative impact of the movies, Duke referred to as "protest films," he set out to make a series of patriotic films. The four motion pictures he chose to do based on their positive political content were *Flying Leathernecks* and *Operation Pacific*, released in 1951, *Big Jim McLain*, released in 1952, and *Jet Pilot*, released in 1957. All four films were box-office successes.

Big Jim McLain was a specifically anti-Communist film that generated a great deal of attention not only among film-goers, but with motion picture executives and government officials. In the movie Duke plays an FBI investigator working for the House Un-American Activities Committee. When it's learned the Communists are threatening to infiltrate Hawaii, he and his partner are sent to the islands to get evidence against the Red cells that can be used for a documented public hearing.

When the film was released, it instantly sparked the interest of the Federal Bureau of Investigations and specifically J. Edgar Hoover. Hoover was concerned his agency would be perceived by audiences as one that would rob citizens of their civil rights in order to build a case. After reviewing both the completed motion picture and the written screenplay, FBI officials were satisfied the movie had nothing to do with them. They found it to be more the story of the HUAC investigative methods.

Some film critics called *Big Jim McLain* an "embarrassment to the film industry," and many more liberal-minded movie goers

John Wayne starred opposite James Arness in the politcally motivated 1953 film *Big Jim McLain*. *(Courtesy of the Author)*

left the theaters fuming. Although the majority of reviews for the film were poor, it was no less a financial success. At the end of 1952, *Big Jim McLain* ranked among the top thirty highest grossing movies of the year.

Duke's traditional ideas first took root in Iowa. His parents, neighbors, and friends' families were conservative, and though he had at one time considered himself a liberal, he was a registered Republican and was staunchly opposed to excessive taxation, big government, and politicians. He was not shy about sharing his opinion on the subject with those closest to him but was uncomfortable publicly speaking out against any of those areas.

It was that uneasiness that convinced Wayne to turn down the Motion Picture Alliance's initial invitation to be the group's president in 1949. Ward Bond persuaded Wayne to rethink his position, appealing to his patriotism. Bond believed fervently, as did many other members of the motion-picture industry, that the Communist threat was very real and had crept into the making of movies.

"America needs someone like you," Bond told Duke. "The Alliance needs someone of your stature too."

Wayne reconsidered the offer, believing that it would be a great way to stand up for his country. He reasoned that if he could make a difference with the Alliance, he might be able to effect change on a grander scale, but Wayne had no real political ambitions for himself. He was motivated solely to serve the country he loved and to help those in need. One of Wayne's associates said that he was about as "political as a Bengal tiger."

In 1952 Wayne supported Senator Robert Taft of Ohio's run for President of the United States. Taft was against President Franklin Roosevelt's New Deal and the spending that went into funding the program. He was in favor of cutting taxes and putting a cap on government spending. Wayne campaigned heavily for the senator. Dwight D. Eisenhower would take the nomination and become president, but that wouldn't end Duke's relationship with the national political scene.

According to fellow actor Ronald Reagan, "John Wayne represented the true American spirit." The Republican Party capitalized on Wayne's influence in 1968 and called upon the star to open their convention in Miami. He was asked to deliver an inspirational reading rather than the run-of-the-mill invocation. The speech he gave had the desired effect on the cheering crowd. He made it clear to voters that a "true commitment to American values made a difference to all United States citizens."

"This nation," he proudly told delegates, "is more than laws and government. It's an outlook, an attitude." The applause at the conclusion of his speech lasted more than four minutes.

John Wayne served three consecutive terms as president of the Motion Picture Alliance. He was succeeded as the head of the Alliance by Ward Bond. Ronald Reagan would eventually take over as president of the organization, echoing Wayne's

At the request of presidential nominee Richard M. Nixon, John Wayne delivered the opening address at the Republican National Convention in 1968. *(Courtesy of the Author)*

sentiments about love for country and dedication to the American dream.

The controversial investigation conducted by the HUAC resulted in the blacklisting of a large contingency of Hollywood writers, actors, directors, and producers. Many never fully recovered from the social stigma attached to their names and reputation. The HUAC Communist probe also had a negative impact on the Motion Picture Alliance and many of its members. Industry professionals sympathetic to the plight of the individuals who bravely endured being blacklisted accused the Alliance of not only being too compliant with the HUAC but for being anti-labor, anti-Semitic, anti-women, and anti-Negro.

In 1975, thirteen years after the House of Representatives changed the committee's name from HUAC to the Committee on Internal Society, the organization was completely abolished. The Alliance disbanded at the same time.

John Wayne arrived on the other side of the highly publicized "Red Scare" years virtually unscathed. Wayne's liberal peers didn't agree with his involvement with the Alliance, but respected his conservative views and recognized him as a "fair minded individual who was not a reactionary, but a balanced, understanding man." Most of Wayne's fans saw him in the same light. In the midst of a troubled period in U.S. history, Wayne continued to seen by the public as a true American, a symbol of a time when men proved their worth not with words but with action.

"JOHN WAYNE WAS BIGGER THAN LIFE.
IN AN AGE OF FEW HEROES, HE WAS THE
GENUINE ARTICLE. BUT HE WAS MORE
THAN A HERO; HE WAS A SYMBOL OF
MANY OF THE QUALITIES THAT MADE
AMERICA GREAT—THE RUGGEDNESS, THE
TOUGH INDEPENDENCE, THE SENSE OF
PERSONAL CONVICTION AND COURAGE—
ON AND OFF THE SCREEN—THAT REFLECTED
THE BEST OF OUR NATIONAL CHARACTER."

— President Jimmy Carter

FOR LOVE
OF COUNTRY

On the tiny island of Iwo Jima, 660 miles south of Tokyo, 21,000 defenders of Japanese soil burrowed into the volcanic rock and anxiously awaited the American invaders. More than 110,000 Marines were sent in to overtake this key piece of real estate during a definitive battle of World War II.

In 1949 a gifted cast of supporting actors reenacted the bloody engagement in the motion picture *Sands of Iwo Jima*. In one of the most poignant moments of the film, John Wayne's character, John M. Stryker, is holed up in a foxhole with eight members of his outfit. They've been ordered to hold their position and maintain complete silence. The plan is to lure the enemy into a false sense of security and draw them out in the open to be overtaken.

Exhausted and covered with ash, sweat, and sand, Stryker (Wayne) and his men keep their eyes peeled and their heads down. A single star shell rises far in the distance, describing a parabola through the sky and lighting up the faces of the men. Their expressions are a mixture of fear and worry. With the exception of a few bombs exploding, all is quiet on the ground.

Out of the dark, dangerous night a small voice rises up. The feeble cry is from a wounded soldier on the battlefield looking for Sergeant Stryker. Wayne's men look over at him, eagerly waiting for him to respond to his fallen comrade. Members of Stryker's regiment make two attempts to retrieve the injured man, but he stops them before they can act. The seemingly callous behavior enrages one of the Marines nearest Wayne. The young recruit, played by Wayne's friend John Agar, tells his commanding officer that he is going to get the wounded man and if Wayne wants to stop him he'll have to shoot him. Wayne raises his rifle and points it at the Marine. "That's just what I'll do," Wayne says with total resolve. The soldier backs down.

The wounded man on the field continues to cry out. His pleas for help are pitiful. Tears stand in Stryker's eyes as he listens to his friend writhing in pain. Bound by orders and the extreme circumstances, he can't help the soldier. The torment on Stryker's face is heartbreaking.

———

The Sands of Iwo Jima was nominated for four Academy Awards, one of which was for Wayne's performance. He did not win the Oscar for best actor that year, but his contribution did not go unnoticed by his supporters and the readers of *Photoplay Magazine*. Movie-goers voted to give Wayne *Photoplay's* Gold Medal naming him the most popular male star of 1949.

In spite of the viewer accolades, movie critics such as Leonard Wallace and actors such as Gary Cooper and Errol Flynn believed that going to war on the screen more than once could be dangerous for a film career. "You set yourselves up to be an unbelievable hero," Wallace suggested. "No one man wins a war, it's a collective hero-ism. Ticket buyers will cease to be entertained by war pictures starring Wayne for those very reasons."

Moviegoers did not agree with Wallace. Between 1942 and 1949, the average consumer bought more tickets to war movies than any other genre. According to the International Encyclopedia of Film, one-quarter of Hollywood's output

Wayne starred as Sergeant Stryker in *Sands of Iwo Jima* in 1949, receiving an Academy Award nomination. *(Courtesy of the Academy of Motion Picture Arts and Sciences)*

then was war related. Many of those films and documentaries featured John Wayne.

When the United States entered World War II in December of 1941, millions of Americans joined in the fight, including 40,000 motion-picture employees and executives who served in various branches of the Armed Forces. In spite of their absences from Hollywood, business prospered.

Commodities were scarce, but cash was plentiful. Consumers spent their discretionary income at the movies. Theater attendance drastically increased, and 1945 was the most profitable year ever in the film industry's history. Two war pictures that added to the unprecedented earnings that year were *They Were Expendable* and *Back to Bataan*. Both movies starred John Wayne.

Back to Bataan was the first film about the war set in the Philippines. Directed by Edward Dmytrk, the true story centered on U.S. Army Colonel Joseph Madden's work organizing guerrilla fighters against the Japanese. Wayne portrayed war hero Colonel Madden, who also worked as technical advisor on the film.

Back to Bataan was hailed as one of the most factual films to ever come out of Hollywood. It was made in conjunction with the war department and great attention was placed on the detail and authenticity of the actual event. Wayne insisted on the same standard from his own performance. He did not compromise reality by having a double stand in for him when dangerous scenes were being shot. In one part of the story, Colonel Madden is blown out of his dugout. In the re-creation of the scene, so is John Wayne. When the gunpowder discharged, Wayne was thrown several feet. He was bruised, but otherwise unhurt. "Colonel Madden didn't have a double when he was thrown out," Wayne told a reporter for *Screenland Magazine*. "It would be an insult for me to use one."

Countless war-themed motion pictures were made to remind movie goers what the fighting was all about: the preservation of American culture and history. No Hollywood star embodied the ideal soldier, sailor, or pilot like John Wayne. Audiences found him so convincing in the war films he appeared in that his name and likeness was thought of as the quintessential image of the brave military man.

Franklin D. Roosevelt's presidential media liaison, Lowell Mellett, felt support from actors like John Wayne was essential to the war effort. Wayne was an established cowboy hero when the Office of War Information (OWI) was created on June 13, 1942. The organization's main objective was to enhance public understanding of the war at home and abroad. The organization sought out filmmakers and stars to help achieve this objective. The OWI wanted movie producers and actors to consider if the films they were involved in would help win the war.

One of the films Republic Studios felt contributed a great deal to the war effort was *Flying Tigers*. Released in October 1942, the movie was the story of a band of American mercenaries called

John Wayne, above, cast as the U. S. Army officer who organizes guerrilla warfare to continue the defense of the island after the fall of Bataan. Far left: Ducky Louie enacts one of the film's most dramatic moment when he tries to halt the hanging of his beloved school principal; left, John Wayne with Anthony Quinn portraying an officer in the Philippine Scouts.

Movie Stars Parade Magazine highlighted Wayne's performance in *Back to Bataan*. *(Courtesy of the Author)* upon by China to help fight the Japanese two years before Pearl Harbor. In what would be the first of many of his patriotic films, John Wayne played the captain of a squadron of pilots. Audiences craving good news from the war front were encouraged by the pictures message and quickly identified Wayne as a hero.

He starred in two other war pictures in 1942, *Reunion in France* and *Pittsburgh*. The politicians who chaired the OWI had strong objections to both films; they felt they created a more favorable picture of the United States's enemies than necessary. In spite of the criticism from the government agency, the films were financial successes.

Wayne's fans and the OWI credited him with helping to keep America's spirit up during World War II. Wayne believed so thoroughly in the work he was doing and had such a deep love for his country and the military men fighting for freedom, that the man and the roles were inseparable.

Wayne's string of war films during the 1940s cemented his reputation as a patriot with American audiences, and Wayne's noble image extended beyond the borders of the United States. In 1974, Japanese Emperor Hirohito visited the country and specifically asked to meet "the man who personified the American spirit, John Wayne."

Wayne was gracious and humble about the way the public saw him and he was indebted to the movie business for the opportunities given to him. "In a way, I guess I feel about

motion pictures something like the Leathernecks (WWII
Marine aviators) do about the Marines," Wayne said in a 1951
interview for a *Los Angeles Citizen's* newspaper column.

> That's putting it too strongly, of course. To the Marines, the great-
> est thing in the world is simply a fact of being a member of the
> fightinest crew that ever bore arms.
>
> A Marine will go through 57 varieties of hell, and maybe even
> like it, because that's the tradition of the corps. We can use a lot of
> that spirit in our business. We've got every reason to be proud of
> motion pictures, and for being associated with the making of them.
> We should express that pride in giving our best in the way of acting
> and technical performances, and in conducting ourselves as self-
> respecting members of a highly respected industry. And if I sound
> like I'm on a soap box, that's the way I feel about the movies.

According to several Wayne biographers, Duke was honored
to have had a chance to serve his country via films but was
unhappy about not being able to join the military. His attempts
to do so were thwarted not only by Republic Studios president
Herbert Yates, who refused to release him from his contract
with the studio, but by the Armed Forces itself. Yates success-
fully argued that Wayne's talents could be put to better use
boosting the morale of the American people by making movies.
The military agreed and allowed Yates to put off Wayne's
enlistment and have him reclassified as 2-A, "deferring in support of national health, safety, or interest."

In addition to helping the war effort through his motion pictures, Wayne engaged in regional publicity tours to sell war bonds, promote scrap-metal drives, and remind Americans of the "boys in the battle." In late 1943, Wayne traveled overseas with a U.S.O. camp show to help improve the moral of the troops. When he returned in early 1944, he gave an interview to the *Los Angeles Herald Examiner* and praised the men on the Pacific front.

What the guys down there need are letters and cigars. More snapshots, phonograph needles, and radios. Their G.I. Bands need reeds, strings and orchestrations. And if you have any cigarette lighters, send 'em along. Otherwise the war is going pretty well—except for such nuisances as heat, rain, monotony, and Japs.

I can't say it enough. Those guys are in a war that's not only fighting, but work and sweat. They're where 130 degrees is a cool day, where they scrape flies off, where matches melt in their pockets and Jap daisy cutter bombs take legs off at the hips. They'll build stages out of old crates, then sit in mud and rain for three hours waiting for someone like me to say, "Hello, Joe."

World War II ended in 1945, but Hollywood continued to make movies about the experience. *Operation Pacific* and *Flying Leathernecks* were popular post-war films. *Operation Pacific* placed Wayne in command of a submarine and *Flying Leathernecks* as the leader of an aviation team. Both accurately

Duke Wayne believed strongly that as a movie star he should help contribute to the war effort. Here he is at one of his many U.S.O. appearances. *(Courtesy of the Academy of Motion Picture Arts and Sciences)*

depicted the hazards of war and the price of freedom. Both were
on the Hollywood trade paper's list of the most profitable
movies of 1951.

Duke's rugged, patriotic persona in the numerous war movies
he made and his willingness to tour the hot spots of the war to
visit wounded soldiers prompted the American Legion to
acknowledge his sacrifice. In 1948, they presented Wayne with
an award for serving the country in the proper manner in
motion pictures.

The influence Wayne had on America, especially during
World War II, would be recognized on a grander scale nearly
thirty years later. In 1979, Wayne was awarded the
Congressional Medal of Honor. The gold medal was inscribed
with three words: "John Wayne, American."

————————

"JOHN WAYNE COULD HAVE BEEN ONE
OF THE BEST DIRECTORS IN HOLLYWOOD,
IF GOD HAD NOT MADE HIM A STAR."

— *Cliff Lyons, Second Unit Director on* The Alamo

WAYNE'S ALAMO

When young Duke Morrison walked onto his first movie set in late 1926, he never imagined he would ever be more than one of the members of the studio's prop department. He had been an avid fan of movies, and in particular of the matinee-idol cowboys of his youth—the men who reenacted the exploits of lawmen and outlaws preserving the myth of the Wild West. If Duke could have envisioned himself as a regular part of motion pictures at all, it would have been as a film cowboy.

As fate would have it, Duke was given the opportunity to portray a series of on-screen wranglers. Movie-goers in the mid-1920s called them "knights of the prairie." Duke excelled as a prairie knight but he was not content to solely be an actor on horseback. After years of studying his craft, he sought to branch out into producing and directing. He wanted to make movies that would prolong the life of the American West in the public's imagination. He specifically wanted to make a movie about the small band of men who sacrificed their lives at the Alamo. Wayne felt that everything he had experienced in his young career had prepared him for making that film—and he would not be satisfied until he realized that goal.

The mission known as the Alamo, where Santa Anna's army battled a band of patriots in the 1830s, is located in the heart of San Antonio, Texas. The fight over the Alamo lasted thirteen days in late 1835 and claimed the lives of 180 people, including Davy Crockett, Jim Bowie, and Colonel William Travis. To many Americans, the Alamo became a symbol of unbending courage and patriotism.

John Wayne, fascinated with the true tale of heroes fighting a dictatorship, got the idea for a movie about the Alamo in 1949 when he happened to be discussing the Texans' resolve with a friend. Inspired and determined to make the film, Wayne struggled for ten years to find a studio willing to bankroll his vision.

He initially thought that Republic would back the venture. He was a contract player with the studio and Herbert Yates, the president of Republic Pictures, had agreed to let Wayne produce several movies of his choosing. Yates and Wayne, however, disagreed about the costs of the production and where the movie would be filmed. The difference of opinion ultimately resulted in the actor and studio parting company.

But Wayne's concerns extended beyond budget and location. He wanted to personally oversee every aspect of his dream project from choosing the camera angles to choreographing battle scenes. He intended *The Alamo* to be a grand epic Western and a tribute to the men who lost their lives for Texas's independence.

Over the course of seven years, Wayne presented the concept of the film to several studio executives. If he had been willing to compromise his vision for the movie, he could have been granted the money early on to produce the picture. Paramount Pictures and 20th Century Fox liked the idea, but had their own ideas about the film that did not include Wayne as a director. Duke refused to negotiate. In 1956 he decided to sign a deal with United Artists. The studio agreed to partially fund the film on the condition that Wayne take one of the starring roles. After careful consideration he accepted their terms.

Wayne spent $2.5 million to build a set of the Alamo mission turned fort. More than a million bricks were made and used in the construction of the location. The building, located just 130 miles west of the historic Alamo site, took two years to complete.

For Wayne's grand view of the project to be fully realized, he needed more money. The screenplay, written by James Grant, who also penned *Sands of Iwo Jima*, contained spectacular, and therefore expensive, action sequences. In order to make the movie as realistic as possible and stay true to the script, Wayne estimated the film's budget at $12 million.

Almost from the moment Wayne conceived the idea for the motion picture, he was butting heads with industry leaders and business professionals. He argued with studio bosses on artistic matters, with financial managers over the expense of the film, and with friends over his casting choices. None of those conflicts could persuade him to sacrifice his view of the material. He effectively campaigned for the bulk of the money he needed to film the movie and mortgaged his home and personal property to make up the difference.

The fifty-one-year-old Wayne always saw himself acting in one of the minor roles in the film. He believed a smaller part would give him the time needed to direct. The conditions United Artist laid out forced him to rethink the casting, however. He felt he was too old to play Jim Bowie or Colonel Travis, which left the only other lead character, Davy Crockett. Actors Richard Widmark and Laurence Harvey accepted offers to star as Bowie and Travis, thus Wayne prepared for the Davy Crockett role.

Organizing the numerous facets of a multi-million-dollar production was overwhelming, but Wayne was determined that he alone should be in charge. "I do believe that one man should serve as producer and director," he told Hedda Hopper in a

Wayne starred as Colonel Davy Crockett in the 1960 film, *The Alamo*, which he also produced and directed. *(Courtesy of Virginia Shahan, owner of Alamo Village in Bracketville, Texas)*

1947 interview. "Making a film is like painting a picture. If you were having your portrait painted you wouldn't have one artist do your eyes, another your nose, and still a third your mouth. That's why I think as nearly as possible, production control should be centered on the talents of a single individual."

Wayne's ideas about filmmaking were strongly influenced by his mentor John Ford. "He's a director whose judgment you can trust implicitly," Duke bragged in an interview for the *Chicago Tribune* in 1952:

> When I'm working under him all I ask is, "What kind of clothes do you want me to wear?" The rest I leave up to him. He directs instinctively, rather than sticking to a book of set rules. If a scene comes off in a different manner than he'd planned he's liable to say, "Print it!" He knows quality when he sees it.

Wayne not only adopted Ford's take-charge attitude but his use of natural backgrounds. The vast landscape surrounding *The Alamo* set was majestic—not unlike the Monument Valley location used in *Stagecoach*. Wayne wanted the backdrop of the Texas desert to point up the isolation of the action.

Before principle photography began on *The Alamo*, Wayne was scheduled to appear in two other Westerns, *Rio Bravo* and *The Horse Soldiers*. *Rio Bravo* also starred Dean Martin, Angie Dickinson, and Rick Nelson. Directed by Howard Hawks, the movie focused on the efforts of a small-town sheriff, played by

Wayne, who was working to save its citizens from a wealthy land baron set on taking over the territory. In *The Horse Soldiers*, directed by John Ford, Wayne played opposite William Holden. Both movies were commercial hits, generating more than $20 million in ticket sales.

Any downtime Wayne had while working on *Rio Bravo* and *The Horse Soldiers* was spent laboring over the pre-production of *The Alamo*. An art director, cinematographer, and production supervisor were hired. Wayne reviewed the screenplay again and again, collaborating with James Grant on the script rewrites. On August 22, 1959, all was in place to begin filming.

The cast and crew assembled on *The Alamo* set totaled more than 350 people. After a priest blessed the production, cameras started to roll. In addition to the number of people working on the film, there were 1,400 horses and the largest herd of Texas Longhorn cattle ever used in motion pictures. Handling such an enormous staff and managing the collection of cattle and horses was a daunting task. The corrals used to hold the animals covered 500 acres and it cost the production $3,300 a day in feed.

The set seemed to attract chaos. Actor Richard Widmark proved to be difficult to work with. A fire broke out on the set, destroying many of Wayne's files and documents associated with the film. One of the cast members broke a foot and another was murdered by her boyfriend. Duke's dedication in the project spurred him on as he addressed each troubling

The Alamo set, located in Bracketville, Texas, was built under Wayne's supervision. The set has been expanded and several movies have been filmed there. (Courtesy of Virginia Shahan, owner of Alamo Village in Bracketville, Texas)

situation. Then, in the midst of the organized chaos, John Ford stopped by to give his protégé moral support.

John Ford was not content simply to observe the film being made. By nature he was a director and as such could not resist the temptation to start directing. Wayne gave his old friend a great deal of leeway as he offered his assistance around the set. He felt he owed him a debt of gratitude and was willing, for awhile at least, to let him interject his own thoughts and artistic impressions.

The tension on the set was palpable. All those involved with the project wondered if Ford was taking over. After assuring the cast and crew that he was still in charge of the production, Wayne graciously asked Ford to help him out with filming some additional action sequences. Ford agreed.

For years film historians and movie critics have speculated that Ford, not Wayne, directed the battle scenes that appeared in the movie. Ford denied any significant contribution to the production and added that "none of the footage he shot made it into the film at all."

By mid-December 1959, Wayne had finished filming and began the time-consuming task of sifting through the 568,000 feet of film he had shot. Stuart Gilmore was the editor of the picture. He and Wayne spent six months getting the movie prepared for release. The final product was ready to show on October 22, 1960. A million dollars was spent nationwide to promote the film. Theaters were flooded with patrons when the movie debuted.

Reviews for *The Alamo* were mixed. Many thought the three-hour-twelve-minute run time was too long. Some felt Wayne's performance was wooden and unconvincing. Still others were impressed with Wayne's directing and found the battle scenes to be compelling and unforgettable. Wayne's colleagues weighed in with their opinions as well. Director George Stevens, who directed *Shane* and *Giant,* called the movie a "modern classic." John Ford proclaimed *The Alamo* was "the greatest picture I'd ever seen."

The Alamo grossed more than $17 million in a couple of months, and when the Academy Award nomination for the year were announced, the film was listed in the category of best picture. The epic story also received nominations for best cine-matography, sound, musical score, and film editing. Chill Willis, one of the movie's costars, got a nod for best supporting actor. Wayne was thrilled with the recognition and invested $750,000 in an ad campaign to convince the voting members of the academy to give the film the top award.

Ultimately, the only Oscar the film was awarded was for sound. Among the other accolades *The Alamo* received was a Golden Globe for best original score, a Laurel Award for top action performances by John Wayne and Chill Willis, and the Western Heritage Award for best picture.

In 1959 Wayne told a Hollywood reporter that *"The Alamo would tell what his future held."* The critical and box-office success of the film proved to the world and to Duke that he was more than a cowboy-soldier star. Ten years after the first release of the film, United Artists re-released the motion picture. Since then it has become one of the most profitable movies in Hollywood history.

Wayne's position of respect in the film industry and the struggles he endured to realize his goals were synonymous with the legends he portrayed. As Davy Crockett in *The Alamo*, Wayne delivered a speech that could very well have been a statement about both his personal and professional pursuits.

It was like I was empty. Well, I'm not empty anymore. That's what's important, to feel useful in this old world, to hit a lick against what's wrong for what's right even though you get walloped. Now I may sound like a Bible beater yelling up a revival at a river crossing camp meeting, but that don't change the truth none. There's right and there's wrong. You got to do one or the other. You do the one and you're living. You do the other and you may be walking around, but you're dead as a beaver hat.

John Wayne directed only one other film in his career—*The Green Berets*—in 1968.

———————

EPILOGUE: CELEBRATING DUKE

Over John Wayne's fifty-plus-year career in the motion picture industry he received numerous awards. He cherished the Academy Award he won in 1969, but was extremely proud of the honor bestowed upon him by the Foreign Press Association, which awarded him the "Henrietta" for being the most popular film star by overseas fans from 1951 to 1956. Ticket sales proved Wayne was a popular actor worldwide and the Foreign Press Association confirmed his standing at the box office.

As the *Hollywood Reporter* wrote on February 16, 1953:

John Wayne and Susan Hayward were voted the most popular film stars overseas by the fans of more than 50 countries in the third annual poll conducted by the Foreign Press Association of Hollywood. The "Henrietta" awards were presented to the winners Saturday night at a banquet in the Club Del Mar Santa Monica, with William Holden and Greer Garson making the presentations and Vincent Price serving as emcee.

Nine special award plaques for outstanding 1952 achievement also were presented to Bette Davis, Roy Rogers, Jimmy McHugh, Susan Whitney, LeRoy Prinz, Olivia de Havilland, Richard Burton, Jane Darwell and Massaichi Nagata. The latter heads the Daiel company of Japan which produced "Rasho-mon."

Winners of International Stardom Awards as the stars of tomorrow were Betta St. John, Mary Murphy, Julia Adams, Robert

Wagner, Dawn Addams, Richard Wesson and Barbara Ruick.

Four other awards were presented for outstanding motion pictures—"The Greatest Show on Earth," "Hans Christian Andersen," "High Noon" and "It's a Big Country."

John "Duke" Wayne, who established himself as a first-rate performer and embodied the American hero in more than 175 movies, died when he was seventy-two, passing away on June 11, 1979, after a fifteen-year battle with cancer. Friends and fans around the world mourned the Duke, and some wrote tributes to the star. Soon-to-be President of the United States Ronald Reagan penned the following article, which was published in *Reader's Digest* in October 1979.

"Unforgettable John Wayne," By Ronald Reagan

We called him DUKE and he was every bit the giant off screen he was on. Everything about him—his stature, his style, his convictions—conveyed enduring strength, and no one who observed his struggle in those final days could doubt that strength was real. Yet there was more. To my wife, Nancy, "Duke Wayne was the most gentle, tender person I ever knew."

In 1960, as president of the Screen Actors' Guild, I was deeply embroiled in a bitter labor dispute between the Guild and the motion picture industry. When we called a strike, the film industry unleashed a series of stinging personal attacks on me—criticism my wife found difficult to take.

At 7:30 one morning the phone rang and Nancy heard Duke's booming voice: "I've been readin' what these damn columnists are saying about Ron. He can take care of himself, but I've been worrying about how all this is affecting you." Virtually every morning until the strike was settled several weeks later, he phoned her. When a mass meeting was called to discuss settlement terms, he left a dinner party so that he could escort Nancy and sit at her side. It was, she said, like being next to a force bigger than life.

Countless others were also touched by his strength. Although it would take the critics forty years to recognize what John Wayne was, the movie-going public knew all along. In this country and around the world, Duke was the most popular box-office star of all time. For an incredible twenty-five years he was rated at or around the top in box-office appeal.

His films grossed $700 million—a record no performer in Hollywood has come close to matching. Yet John Wayne was more than an actor; he was a force around which films were made. As Elizabeth Taylor Warner stated last May when testifying in favor of the special gold medal Congress struck for him: "He gave the whole world an image of what an American should be."

JOHN WAYNE FILMOGRAPHY

1926

The Great K&A Train Robbery

Bardelys the Magnificent

Brown of Harvard

1927

The Drop Kick

Annie Laurie

1928

Hangman's House

Four Sons

Mother Machree

1929

The Forward Pass

Salute

Words & Music

Noah's Ark

The Black Watch

Speak Easy

1930

Cheer Up & Smile

Rough Romance

Born Reckless

Men Without Women

The Big Trail

1931

Maker of Men

Range Feud

The Deceiver

Arizona

Three Girls Lost

Girls Demand Excitement

1932

Haunted Gold

The Big Stampede

That's My Boy

Ride Him, Cowboy

The Hollywood Handicap

The Hurricane Express

Lady and Gent

Two-Fisted Law

Texas Cyclone

The Shadow of the Eagle

The Voice of Hollywood No. 13

1933

Sagebrush Trail

College Coach

Riders of Destiny

Baby Face

The Life of Jimmy Dolan

His Private Secretary

Somewhere in Sonora

Central Airport

The Three Musketeers

The Telegraph Trail

The Man from Monterey

1934

'Neath the Arizona Skies

The Lawless Frontier

The Trail Beyond

The Star Packer

Randy Rides Alone

The Man from Utah

Blue Steel

West of the Divide

The Lucky Texan

1935

Lawless Range

The New Frontier

Westward Ho

Paradise Canyon

The Dawn Rider

The Desert Trail

Rainbow Valley

Texas Terror

1936

Conflict

Sea Spoilers

Winds of the Wasteland

The Lonely Trail

King of the Pecos

The Lawless Nineties

The Oregon Trail

1937

Born to the West

Adventure's End

Idol of the Crowds

I Cover the War

California Straight Ahead!

1938

Red River Range

Sante Fe Stampede

Overland Stage Riders

Pals of the Saddle

1939

Allegheny Uprising

New Frontier

Wyoming Outlaw

Three Texas Steers

The Night Riders

Stagecoach

1940

Seven Sinners

The Long Voyage Home

Three Faces West

Dark Command

1941

The Shepherd of the Hills

Lady from Louisiana

A Man Betrayed

1942

Reunion in France

Pittsburgh

The Flying Tigers

In Old California

The Spoilers

Reap the Wild Wind

Lady for a Night

1943

In Old Oklahoma

A Lady Takes a Chance

1944

Tall in the Saddle

The Fighting Seabees

1945

Dakota

They Were Expendable

Back to Bataan

Flame of the Barbary Coast

1946

Desert Command

Without Reservation

1947

Tycoon

Angel and the Badman

1948

Wake of the Red Witch

Red River

Fort Apache

3 Godfathers

1949

Sands of Iwo Jima

She Wore a Yellow Ribbon

The Fighting Kentuckian

1950

Rio Grande

1951

Flying Leathernecks

Operation Pacific

1952

Miracle in Motion

Big Jim McLain

The Quiet Man

1953

Hondo

Island in the Sky

Trouble Along the Way

1954

The High and the Mighty

1955

Blood Alley

The Sea Chase

1956

The Searchers

The Conqueror

1957

Legend of the Lost

Jet Pilot

The Wings of Eagles

1958

The Barbarian and the Geisha

I Married a Woman

1959

The Horse Soldiers

Rio Bravo

1960

North to Alaska

The Alamo

1961

10 del Texas

The Comancheros

1962

How the West Was Won

The Longest Day

Hatari

The Man Who Shot Liberty Valance

1963

Donovan's Reef

McLintock

1964

Circus World

1965

In Harm's Way

The Greatest Story Ever Told

The Sons of Katie Elder

1966

El Dorado

Cast a Giant Shadow

1967

The War Wagon

1968

Hellfighters

The Green Berets

1969

The Undefeated

True Grit

1970

Rio Lobo

Chisum

1971

Big Jake

1972

The Cowboys

Cancel My Reservation

1973

Cahill U.S. Marshall

The Train Robbers

1974

Mc Q

1975

Brannigan

Rooster Cogburn

1976

The Shootist

BIBLIOGRAPHY

Magazines

Farm Journal, April 1939.

LIFE, November 11, 1940.

Look, October 6, 1942.

Modern Screen, July 1939.

Motion Picture, November 1940.

Motion Picture Magazine, February 1931.

Movie Stars Parade, January 1946.

Picturegoer, August 25, 1951

Screenland, May 1945.

TIME, March 3, 1952.

TIME, October 12, 1942.

Newspapers

Chicago Tribune, February 13, 1949.

Glendale News Press, July 12, 1922; June 18, 1925; November 20, 1978; June 12, 1979.

Glendale Daily News, November 17, 1988.

Hollywood Reporter, February 12, 1951.

The Ledger Glendale, May 30, 1979.

Los Angeles Citizens News, October 5, 1951.

Los Angeles Daily News, February 16, 1953.

Los Angeles Examiner, October 31, 1944; November 1, 1944; March 24, 1949.

Los Angeles Times, November 1, 1944; January 26, 1990; February 18, 1990.

Saturday Evening Post, December 23, 1950; July/August 1979.

Books

Ford, Dan. *Pappy: The Life of John Ford*. Cambridge: Da Capo Press, 1998.

Fox-Sheinwold, Patricia. *Gone But Not Forgotten*. New York: Bell Publishing, 1958.

George-Warren, Holly. *Cowboy*. Pleasantville: Reader's Digest Association, 2002.

Hardy, Phil. *The Overlook Film Encyclopedia: The Western*. Woodstock: Overlook Press, 1983.

Heide, Robert and Gilman, John. *Box-Office Buckaroos*. New York: Abbeville Press Publishers, 1973.

Katz, Ephraim. *The Film Encyclopedia*. New York: Perigee Books, 1979.

Manvell, Roger. *The International Encyclopedia of Film*. New York: Bonanza Books, 1972.

Place, J. A. *The Western Films of John Ford*. Secaucas: Citadel Press, 1973.

Roberts, Randy and Olson, James. *John Wayne American*. New York: Free Press, 1995.

Rothel, David. *An Ambush of Ghosts*. Madison: Empire Publishing, 1990.

Wiley, Mason and Bona, Damien. *Inside Oscar: The Unofficial History of the Academy Awards*. New York: Ballantine Books, 1987.

Wills, Garry. *John Wayne's America*. New York: Simon & Schuster, 1998.

Zolotow, Maurice. *Shooting Star: A Biography of John Wayne*. New York: Pocket Book Press, 1974.

Websites

www.imdb.com

www.johnwaynebirthplace.org

www.lonepinefilmhistorymuseum.org

www.nndb.com

www.san.beck.org

www.silentsaregolden.com

www.wildestwesterns.com

INDEX

Page numbers in italics indicate photographs.

ABOUT THE AUTHORS

Howard Kazanjian is an award-winning producer and entertainment executive who has been producing feature films and television programs for more than twenty-five years. While vice president of production for Lucasfilm Ltd., he produced two of the highest grossing films of all time: *Raiders of the Lost Ark* and *Star Wars: Return of the Jedi*. He also managed production of another top-ten box-office hit, *The Empire Strikes Back*. Some of his other notable credits include *The Rookies*, *Demolition Man*, and the two-hour pilot and first season of *J.A.G.*

Chris Enss is an award-winning screenwriter who has written for television, short subject films, live performances, and for the movies. She is the author of numerous books on the western experience, including *Hearts West: True Stories of Mail-Order Brides on the Frontier*, *How the West Was Worn: Bustles and Buckskins on the Wild Frontier*, *Buffalo Gals: Women of Buffalo Bill's Wild West show*, and *The Doctor Wore Petticoats: Women Physicians of the Old West*. She collaborated with Howard Kazanjian on *Happy Trails: A Pictorial Celebration of the Life and Times of Roy Rogers and Dale Evans*. Together they are working on the movie version of *The Cowboy and the Senorita*, their biography of Western stars Roy Rogers and Dale Evans.